MARIE'S MOMENTS

A COLLECTION OF COLUMNS
BY MARIE MACDONALD

Selected by Charles Pearson

Printed in the United States of America by Mennonite Press, Inc.,
Newton, Kansas 67114

ISBN 1-880-652-36-6

Cover illustration and design by Sara Quinn
Copyedited by Julie Mah

Marie MacDonald
1910-1992

FOREWORD

It was not long after Marie MacDonald's death that the staff at Active Aging began hearing from some of her many friends and admirers. They wanted to know when we were going to publish a collection of her columns. Not whether. When. They took it for granted that there would be no doubt in our minds about the aptness and appeal of such a book. And they were right.

So, here it is.

It was not easy to decide just how to go about this. Marie had written thousands of words in her Moments column. There wasn't room for them all. So we began by looking them all up and reading them carefully. A few we eliminated because they seemed dated. That done, we faced a dilemma.

When Marie started the column, she said what she wanted to do was write about individuals, and do it in such a way that people who were strangers would feel they were meeting one another through the column. And such was her sensitivity and liking for humanity in general that she was able to accomplish just that.

Unfortunately, it was those very parts of her column that we felt we must omit in this book. Marie was not a name-dropper. She knew most of the "important" people, but she was no more impressed by them than by anyone else, and most of the names in the column were of neighbors and friends and fellow retirees of The Eagle-Beacon and people from her church and others that she met on her busy rounds.

She wrote little anecdotes about them. Some were amusing. Some were touching. All made good reading at the time. But our reasoning was that after so much time had passed, most of the readers of this book would be unlikely to recognize many of the names, and that the incidents weren't the right stuff to stand alone. It was a judgment call. I hope it was not a bad one.

What remains are the more general aspects of Marie's Moments: her philosophizing, her story-telling about episodes in her active and varied life, her observations about what was going on around her, all told in her unique style of unadorned language and genuine affection for people.

Pulling the book together would not have been possible without the help of a number of people, among them Bill Handy and his associates in the Development Department at The Wichita Eagle. Becky Funke, editor of Active Aging, helped with the editing and did all the initial typesetting. Ruth Viets, president of the Active Aging governing board, proofread all the copy and saved us from ourselves again and again. Bill Stanhope and Bob Hobson, members of the Active Aging board, negotiated the business aspects of the book with The Eagle. And Nancy Avery, one of Marie's closest friends, graciously consented to contribute the introduction.

I am grateful to all of them for the contributions they have made, but don't blame them for any faults.

That responsibility is mine alone. As for me, I'm thankful for the chance to have done the editing.

In re-reading all of Marie's columns, I felt that I was again spending a good many pleasant hours in her company, and that's an enviable experience.

Charles Pearson
Wichita, Summer 1994

INTRODUCTION

This collection of columns from Active Aging offers only a brief insight into Marie MacDonald. She was a woman of many talents — actress, radio/TV personality, newspaper writer, editor and columnist, historical researcher, volunteer. She wrote scripts, gave speeches, re-created characters from history, and enjoyed several careers during her 82 years.

As a young woman, she and husband King (she always called him Mac) traveled the country in "circle stock," performing melodramas and comedies. Having been impressed with the friendliness of Wichita audiences, the MacDonalds chose to make their home in Wichita when World War II forced stock theater to close.

Biographies in several Who's Who publications list among Marie's professional pursuits: women's editor of The Wichita Beacon; director of women's activities and broadcaster at KFBI and KARD-TV; assistant program director at KFH Radio; and feature writer at The Wichita Eagle-Beacon, to name a few.

While she spent many years in communications, she never really left the theater. For the American Red Cross, she portrayed Clara Barton. As ambassador for the Old Cowtown Museum, she was Julia Munger, Rea Woodman, Harriet Fisher and Victoria Murdock. For the Women From Wichita History program at the Wichita-Sedgwick County Historical Museum in conjunction with Women's History Month, she presented one of her favorite sketches as Rea Woodman. All that from a woman whose biography states that she never had the opportunity to complete her high school education!

Marie never stopped learning. She was a woman of many interests. While she enjoyed delving into Wichita's past, she also was active in her adopted city's day-to-day life. She belonged to many professional and social organizations — and many of them recognized her through the years with awards and honors for her achievements. The Wichita City Council even declared a Marie MacDonald Day.

She loved gardening, she loved books (especially murder mysteries), she loved her church, she loved people — and she loved life. She filled every minute, yet she always had time if someone needed help. As she explored new ideas, she would try them out on a friend. Her telephone calls would always begin, "Do you have a minute?" and one minute would turn into many.

Friends say that what made Marie important was not what she did but rather who she was.

Anyone who ever met her came away with at least one "Marie story" to tell. Many of those stories dealt with Marie's ability to laugh at herself, as her sense of humor was one of her most endearing qualities. Once, on a particularly hot summer day when she was portraying Mrs. Munger at Old Cowtown, a visitor asked how she could wear such heavy clothing, yet look so cool and self-assured.

With a little smile, Marie lifted her Victorian hat to reveal her secret — an ice bag.

Marie died Christmas Eve 1992. Although she was known widely for her many achievements, friends defined her as "a woman for all seasons," a "consummate professional," an "articulate communicator." Common words seem inadequate to describe this uncommon woman.

If pressed to choose one characteristic which

summed up Marie MacDonald, however, all would agree that she was a friend.

Nancy Avery, May 1994

Marie as Victoria Murdock at Old Cowtown Museum.

x

IN THE BEGINNING...

January 1981

Scarlett O'Hara and I have something in common. We are both put-ter off-ers.

I volunteered to write a column for Active Aging. In fact I asked to do one. I had all these neat, lofty ideas I wanted to share with you.

I kept waiting for the perfect time to write — when everything was quiet with no interruptions, a time that never came.

So, folks, I need help.

I do know what I would like this column to be, and I need your help for that.

I'd like it to be a caring and sharing column where people our age (I hate labels, don't you?) can come to a new appreciation of ourselves and each other. Not only a place to share our gripes and disillusionment ... but also a place to rekindle our zest for living, investigate new ideas, new experiences and new attitudes.

For years I worked at The Wichita Eagle and Beacon, but it wasn't until I retired and started going to the E & B retirees breakfasts that I really learned to know those people to whom I had been saying a casual, daily, "Hi, how are you?" They are great, and we have such fun talking about how much better "we" did things.

These are some of the people I want you to meet and, I'm sure you know a lot of great people, too. So, let's be name-droppers and share acquaintances. We will be rich just knowing that people our age are the luckiest people in the world because we've learned to appreciate the important things in life.

As I write, 1981 is still an unopened book, its pages unblemished by disappointments, tragedy and grief. Very few of us will mourn the passing of 1980 with its rising inflation, political hassles, heat, volcanoes and crime in the streets.

But let's face it folks, a new year won't change all the ills of the world.

I remember another year back in the 1940s. We had come out of the Depression, when few people could afford the necessities of life, into a war when those necessities were rationed. You had to stand in line for hours hoping the rolls of toilet paper would last until it was your turn. And along with the inconveniences, there was the gnawing anxiety for the American boys on the battlefronts.

At the end of that year, a group of friends gathered at the home of Pete and Leone Lightner for a watch party. As the clock tolled the midnight hour, there were the usual toasts, kisses, tooting of horns and off-key singing of "Auld Lang Syne." Through it all, one young married couple sat together in earnest conversation. Someone called, "Hey, it's New Year's, time to celebrate."

"Oh, we are celebrating," the pretty young wife called back. "We have just been naming all the good things we shared this past year."

With this in mind, let's remember the good things we can share. Maybe that will help 1981 be a better year for us all.

LOOK FOR THINGS THAT WORK

October 1982

Can it really be September?

Of course, by the time these Moments reach you it will be October and time to get out the sweaters and make sure the furnace is ready for another winter.

But for now, the air conditioner is still needed during the day, the flowers are making a comeback, the grass is green and the tomato vines are still producing plenty of red juicy fruit.

This was the one year I could have bragged on my great tomatoes but, as usual, my neighbors have crops better than mine. Oh, well, I have basil and lemon mint.

Getting enough grapes for a gallon of juice meant trying to outwit the birds and, would you believe, two raccoons. My Sheltie tried her best to protect the grapes from the masked bandits and got a bloody nose for her trouble. One evening I saw the two coons sitting on my garage roof helping themselves to the Concords that climb up there.

Taking Charmaine for her evening walk (actually she does the taking) causes me moments of embarrassment. The minute she is out the front door, she barks to let every other dog in the neighborhood know "I'm out," and they all run to their respective fences to yap their greetings. Libby, the cat, usually spends a quiet evening with Marsha's black and white kitty, and tonight the two of them disdainfully watched Charmaine's antics from the hood of my car.

But all the dashing in and out of sprinklers and trying to curb Charmaine from attacking a bicycle pays off for me as we round the corner of Woodrow and Franklin. Mr. Banberry's back yard is the pride of our neighborhood. Starting in the spring with the bulbs, progressing into summer with gorgeous roses, it now is in all the splendrous colors of fall. All of us benefit from the hard work he puts into this beautiful garden.

Another neighbor down the block brought me a copy of the Victorian Society's new cookbook, appropriately titled "Receipts from a Victorian Pantry." How many of you remember when we always called a recipe "receipt"? Rosalyn knows my weakness for cookbooks, and this one is a delight. The foreword is by Lloyd Foltz whose artistic and writing talents are well-known. This is a tiny book full of recipes (excuse me, receipts) from the past and something I'll treasure.

Today I attended the Governor's Conference on "Staying Well in Today's Society." There were special sessions for the "50-Plussers" (that's us). Some of the observations made about being older seem really worthwhile. One of the speakers scolded doctors for telling us to "slow down, take it easy." He feels that is the reason so many older people lose their mobility when they should be "getting off their duff" and doing something to keep the juices flowing.

Rev. George T. Gardner (you've probably heard him on radio or seen him on television) had some good advice for people of all ages. He pointed out the importance of keeping alert, adapting to change.

He thinks we hold on too long to old conceptions of how things should be and suggested we spend more time on "the things that work."

MUDDLE, MEDDLE, MUMBLE

From a series February through April 1981

I would like to discuss a subject suggested by a caller. She works in an office where many people are employed, and she has observed that older people are often bypassed because they have become neglectful.

"Let's face it. As we grow older, we are not as attractive as we once were, so we have to be even more careful of our appearance," she said.

"Also some older people develop habits that turn other people off. They complain too much. They monopolize conversations. They aren't interested in anything but their own ideas."

This woman is in our age bracket, so she isn't putting us down. She just wants to see older people develop to their full potential so that others will find them interesting and of value.

Sure it's difficult to pluck out wild eyebrows when you wear glasses. Poorly fitting dentures make eating a bit difficult. But careful attention to cleanliness and good grooming can do much to improve our physical appearance.

When it comes to those other unattractive habits, well, sometimes we just don't realize we have them. One way to discover our own bad habits is to list those of other people and then ask ourselves, "Am I guilty of that?" One of my many bad habits is finishing other people's sentences. What's yours?

Why not write and tell me what habits you dislike most and what you think we can do to be more "interesting, loveable and nice to be near."

•••••

In reply to our request for ideas on how to eliminate bad habits and improve our attitudes, we received a letter with so many ideas, we'll have to save some for future use.

One writer, who prefers not to have her name used, wants it understood that her thoughts are for the "active" aging, not for those who have "already sunk into oblivion from choice."

To help change the "harsh concept of age," she believes we must first do a complete overhaul of ourselves to remove the "ugly stereotype held up to society as doddering, unkempt individuals who muddle, meddle and mumble ... so let's clean up our act."

We hope that rouses your interest (and perhaps your ire) enough to put you in a state of suspense until we can bring you some of her suggestions for improving our image. Maybe you'd like to respond with some ideas of your own.

•••••

Last month I promised to bring you more suggestions on graceful aging from a reader who has some strong opinions on "talking too much and listening too little. Conversation is a two-way street," she reminds us. "If we feel we must talk, let's make it an interesting discourse. We have lived for quite awhile, through wars, changes in transportation, fashions and lifestyles." With all this background, she feels we shouldn't have to resort to talking so much about how charming we were (in our younger days).

Also, "most of us have friends we love, but we must remember to never exploit them. Some of them drive cars, others don't (either because of finances or the responsibility involved). Therefore don't use your friends just as a means of transportation. There are taxis or social agencies set up to be used for appointments, shopping or pleasure junkets."

SHE WAS A LADY

May 1981

Spring!

Don't you love it?

The good Lord must have had folks like us in mind when he included spring in his creations.

Although I don't dread winter as much as I did when I had to drive to work on icy streets, winter isn't my favorite season. The short days and long evenings tend to remind one of the fleeting years. The drawn drapes, to conserve energy, isolate us from the outside world and make us more aware of our aloneness. It is easy to become depressed, to feel vulnerable, to doubt our immortality.

Then comes spring. The first tender blades of green arrogantly push through the thatch of winter-dead grass. Buds and leaves flesh out the skeletal branches and trunks of trees and shrubs.

And the sight and sound of robins and cardinals bring joy to the soul. Jonquils, tulips and hyacinths ... forsythia, flowering peach and bridal wreath! Such beauty where a short time ago there was drabness.

•••••

The other day a friend of mine said, "I hate that title, 'Senior Citizen,' and I don't want to be called one." I know just how she feels. There is no fringe benefit that makes up for being put into a category that, no matter how you soften it, still means "old."

Young people feel the same way about being called "kid." To them, it signifies inexperience, inability to handle adult situations. But they have an alternative we don't have. In just a few years they will be out of their present

category. Which reminds me of something I heard someone say ... maybe it was George Burns. Someone asked
him how he liked being old. He replied, "I like it fine when
I consider the alternative." We have run out of categories.

But there should be some guidelines suggesting the
plateau of our lives, some sort of preparation that cush-
ions the shock of hearing someone say, "Senior Citizen"
(or worse "Old Lady") and realize they mean You.

Then along comes Lillian Gish to remind us that age
has its rewards too. Did you see her on the Academy
Awards show? Wasn't she great? The following day I
attended a luncheon and was seated next to a young man
who was talking about the show. He laughed at the
stringy hair and ridiculous clothing worn by some of the
young women and then he said, "But did you see that
Miss Gish, wasn't she absolutely fantastic? SHE was a
lady."

IT'S SO DAILY

March 1982

Remember the radio personality (Hattie somebody-
or-other?) who used to complain, "the trouble with
housework, it's so daily."

My sentiments exactly. Dusting, sweeping, dish-
washing, bed-making ... no matter how often you do
those chores, tomorrow they are to do all over again.

Now arranging flowers, cooking ... even sewing ...
are different. They offer a pleasant variety that pleases
the senses. Even an all-over spring cleaning, to have
everything spick-and-span for one day, can be soul satis-
fying. But daily housework — dullsville.

Why all of this to-do over such a mundane subject?

My moment of truth came today when there was no space on my dining room table for my lunch because of newspapers, coupons and scissors for clipping coupons, the daily mail, the dictionary (for crossword puzzles) and playing cards for solitaire. All this covered every inch.

I looked around and, as far as I could see, the clutter matched the table. I am a poor housekeeper!

And worse than that, I don't like housework.

There, I've said it and, if confession is good for the soul, I should be on my way to bliss.

For years I've tricked myself into believing that I really loved housekeeping but that my responsibilities prevented me from being a good housekeeper: my job (once a legitimate excuse); my sister (she doesn't make any demands on me but now and then I do some little something for her); my friends (after all, what good are friends if they are not willing to drop a dustcloth for something important like shopping, bridge, theater or sharing the day's happenings?); or my dog, Charmaine, who deserves a walk or romp in return for her charming company.

I kept telling myself, when I have a few days at home I'll get everything in order. Then I'll be a good housekeeper forever after.

Well, the ideal time came. Almost two weeks of being snowbound.

Perfect, right? Wrongo!

After all, the porch had to be swept and the walks cleared, several times a day, so the mailman, the milkman and the paperboy could get to the door. Charmaine, my Sheltie, and Libby, my liberated tomcat, needed paths in the back yard for certain creature activities. And the snow had to be swept periodically from the place I put out feed for the birds and squirrels.

I even started an exercise program that took a good 45 minutes each day. Then there were the showers, shampoos and decisions of what to wear.

Does that tell you something?

I did manage to keep the dishes washed, the chore I hate most, because a kitchen piled with dirty dishes can put me in a deep depression.

No, I don't like cleaning house. What I do like is having the house clean. So, somehow I must learn to treat housework as I would any other necessary chore — get on with it and get it over with.

As a matter of fact, today, I've done just that; run the sweeper, cleared the clutter. I would have cleaned the bathroom fixtures but I had to stop ... to write this column.

All in all, the two weeks of being housebound have totaled up more positives than negatives.

There was the good friend who knows my aversion to driving in bad weather. She called to see if I needed anything. And it was wonderful hearing from some long-time but seldom-seen friends and catching up on their activities.

And thanks to you good people who called to say you liked the February Moments (I hope today's column doesn't turn you off). And, guess what. Once again I have my Eagle-Beacon delivered to my front door. That is great!

Also, I am so grateful to agencies such as "Give-A-Lift." I've never had to ask for their help but on the day of the worst snowstorm, Give-A-Lift provided my sister transportation to the doctor. And, when she had to wait more than two hours for her appointment (by that time the weather was too bad for the volunteers to drive her home), Give-A-Lift arranged cab transportation for her.

So the stormy weather served to remind me to appreciate the most important things we have in this life … people. Good, friendly, caring people.

ALL DORMANT

April 1982

Many times when I lack inspiration for this column, a bright quip from my neighbor will prod my sluggish mind into productivity. This month, her grandson's observation did the trick.

Matthew is 4-ish, a precocious little fellow whose parents have wisely refrained from using baby talk in their communication with the child. As a result, Matthew often observes and speaks with an adult understanding that is amazing.

He loves to emulate his father's activities. One of his favorite toys is a little lawnmower that permits him to share his father's chore of mowing.

Yesterday was a sunny day with just a hint of spring in the air, and Matthew felt the urge to mow.

So he pushed his little mower around his house until his mother suggested he put on his coat and cap and "go mow the lawn."

Matthew stopped and stood very quietly as if pondering his answer. "Why don't you go?" Mother asked. Matthew shook his head. "Dormant," was his reply.

His mother couldn't argue that outside spring had not yet sent the message to sleeping roots to be up and growing. But she urged, "Oh, why don't you go and look.

Maybe there's some grass you can mow."

But the young man shook his head, "All dormant." That ended the argument.

For the past few months I've been like Matthew's lawn, "all dormant." My creative juices seem to be very sluggish during the dark and dreary days of winter. Outwardly I may be functioning normally, performing the necessary rituals of life. But inwardly I'm curled up in a warm robe and slippers with stacks of interesting reading to recharge my creative batteries, and bowls of popcorn and juicy apples to restore my energy. It is a good thing I don't give in to my fantasy world, or like the bears, I would hibernate from November to April.

Come to think of it, I go through another dormant period when the temperature goes past 100.

Luckily for me, Kansas weather is so changeable that the cold of winter and heat of summer are tempered with spring-like and fall-like days or my creative batteries would be past a recharge.

It was just when my creativity was at a new low ebb that my neighbor shared the latest "Little Matthew's Sayings" with me. If I had a salary to share, a good portion would go to this smart little boy for brightening the dull days for his elders.

There is good news, Matthew. I have just returned from my back yard and, lo, there are little sprigs of green everywhere. The lilacs are ready to burst into leaf, the bulbs are up, and there is evidence of green in the brown thatch of grass. And my dormant grape vines are in need of pruning before they start oozing juice.

Unless winter makes another comeback, soon the yellow of jonquils and forsythia will be harmonizing with the redbud trees and tulips. Kites already compete with the birds for air space, and fat worms are working their way through the cold earth to the warm sun.

By the time you read this, spring will have arrived, and it will be time again to humble ourselves in acknowledgment of the miracle of Easter.

Thank you, Matthew, for nudging me awake to an awareness of God's beautiful earth.

A COUPLE OF OLIVES

September 1982

It is 8:30 in the evening and I'm writing this while seated in a lawn chair in my back yard. Libby, the cat, reclines on the back step and Charmaine, the Sheltie, nuzzles my knee.

Soon the mosquitoes and shadows will drive me indoors, but, for these few moments, I listen to the sweet lonely sounds of passing summer: the off-key concert of the cicada, the crickets and the tree frogs.

After a 94-degree day, a cooling breeze freshens the air and sweetens it with the spicy fragrance of the four-o'clocks and the musky odor of the lilies we call naked ladies. Libby strolls through the herb patch stirring the tangy perfume of sweet basil and sage.

The weeds and grass make my yard untidy by day. But in the twilight it is lovely.

When I started this column, I invited you to be name-droppers. This month I'm going to do a bit of name-dropping of my own because it's the only way I know of paying tribute to two wonderful women who, like ourselves, are actively aging.

By the very nature of my work I've had the good fortune to meet quite a few VIPs. I did a short television show with Ronald Reagan on KARD many years ago, and I interviewed Nancy during a style show in Hollywood; I met Lawrence Welk in Yankton, S.D., when he was the handsome leader of the California Fruit Gum orchestra; and Dorothy Lamour once showed me photos of her children.

Every now and then I take these brief encounters out of my memory bank when I need to bolster my sagging ego. But that's what they were ... brief encounters. I'm sure not one of those people have the faintest recollection of me. And all I know about them is their public image.

But in our own area there are many wonderful people ... persons of affluence but persons whose kindnesses and humanitarian deeds far exceed their monetary achievements.

For this time I mention only two. I've known them longer and they share so many similarities. For one thing they are both named Olive ... Olive Ann Beech and Olive Garvey.

I first knew Olive Ann when I was a newcomer to Wichita and The Wichita Eagle. She probably doesn't remember as I do the day she gently pointed out that her name was spelled BEECH, not Beach (as in Sandy Beach). Somehow she chided me without humiliating me.

I also recall her saying, when asked if she thought a certain venture possible, "You can do anything you think you can."

Her exceptional qualities have made her a "tough" businesswoman without robbing her of the womanly qualities of being a loving mother and a loyal friend whose many acts of kindness often are known only to those lucky enough to be the recipients. She has been an inspiration to many, including me.

I've known Olive Garvey since my early days with the Beacon. In addition to being a wise businesswoman, she has written plays, poetry, travelogues and books. In each is reflected her deep faith. Through the years she has lent her talents and money to various educational and humanitarian endeavors.

One of her latest ventures is the Olive W. Garvey Center for the Improvement of Human Functioning Inc. At a recent groundbreaking ceremony, (only they called it sky breaking), Olive participated in the program.

Although the wind was blowing, not one strand of her beautifully coiffed hair was out of place. She was as trim as a young girl and her smile just as sweet as it must have been many years ago when it captured the heart of Ray Garvey, her late husband.

She astonished the crowd by announcing, "Today is my 89th birthday," then delighted them by adding, "and I've enjoyed every one of them."

After her short and poetic speech, more than 2,000 helium-filled balloons were released. They went hurtling upward, a spectacular and beautiful sight.

Balloons, like so many of our encounters, are beautiful but brief. But beautiful deeds last and last.

THOSE WERE THE DAYS

July 1983

Independence Day falls on Monday this year — a long weekend for some folks. Highways will be filled with cars, many hauling boats, frantically rushing to some away-from-home spot to spend a few hours fishing, boating, water skiing, or golfing, getting a sunburn ... all under the heading of "fun."

Those who can't make it out of town will make do with computer games, swimming at one of the neighborhood pools and broiling hamburgers on the outdoor grill. Some of the more adventurous young folk will take their illegal fireworks and several six-packs out into the country.

Hopefully, the spring moisture will prevent wheat fires from the crackers, and the beer will run out before someone gets the idea it would be fun to play car tag across the fields.

Thinking over the Fourths of my youth, I'm a bit sorry for today's young people. How can they, with their "wheels," their Pac Man games and their sophisticated ideas of fun, relate to the simple pleasures we enjoyed at their age?

Getting ready for the Fourth meant hauling ice from the ice house, one block for the icebox and one block, wrapped carefully in tow sacks, for the hand-cranked ice-cream freezer. A chicken was caught, its neck wrung, and left to drain out the body heat before frying. Potatoes were boiled, fresh eggs hard-cooked and beans put to soak. Pies and cakes kept the old stove busy.

No need to set an alarm. At the break of dawn on the big day, the sound of firecrackers set up a racket that made sleep impossible. Just long enough to get folks out of bed. The rest of the fireworks was saved to climax the day's festivities.

We all dressed up and went to town for the big parade. My brother played the bass horn, my brother-in-law the bass drum. There were speeches, ball games, sack races and a baby contest.

Young girls and their beaus held hands and whispered. Women folk caught up on the gossip, and the men tried to out-do each other on the best way to run the country. We kids played tag, fell down, got dirty and were glad when it was time to go home for lemonade and to snitch bits of ice from the ice-cream bucket. When the freezer handle refused to turn one more time, the whole thing was packed in salt to let the cream "ripen."

Tables were placed in the shadiest spot in the yard (no air conditioning to keep us indoors), and the food was spread out to set our mouths to watering. Until time to fill our plates, we youngsters shooed the flies away with elderberry branches.

When we could eat no more, the ice-cream can was opened and we gathered round to fill our bowls to over-flowing and gorged ourselves some more. I believe today's kids would call it "pigging out."

Those with enough energy played croquet or pitched horseshoes until sunset. Then the great moment of the day arrived. Out came the fireworks!

While I am the first to agree that fireworks are dangerous and should be confined to controlled displays, I'll never forget the thrill of watching skyrockets and twirling sparklers. No display has ever thrilled me more than those fireworks that lit up the sky on the long ago Fourths of July of my childhood.

•••••

18

OTHER MOMENTS TO SAVOR: Spending a day with other members of the Active Aging Advisory Board, guests of Floyd and Norma Souders on their farm near Cheney. These good people have built a museum there: a village, complete with chapel, to house an astounding "past to present" exhibit. There is the telephone office with its old drop-key switchboard; a bank with bullet-proof panels to protect the tellers from hold-ups; a news-paper office with a hand press; a general store and all the other shops necessary to the good life of past generations.

A ride over the farm gave us a view of early-day buffalo wallows. Wild sweet peas and sweet rocket gave promise of a bumper crop of wild flowers to grace Kansas fields. Iced tea, homemade brownies and home-grown strawberries, served by Norma at the "cabin" brought our visit to an end. Thank you, Norma and Floyd, for reminding us that good old-fashioned hospitality is still available in Kansas.

INGATHERING TIME

November 1983

When I was a little girl in Arkansas, we called the fall of the year "ingathering" time. The main crops were in ... corn overflowed the corncrib, the root cellar was filled with potatoes, cabbage and other produce and the pantry was filled with jars of fruits and pickles.

Now it was time to gather in nature's bounty. My cousin Mary and I, with a bucket and tow sack or two, would wend our way down the lane of my uncle's pas-ture, down to the Arkansas River (pronounced Arkansaw in Arkansas) and on to the pecan grove. After gathering our share (leaving enough for the squirrels), we would climb over the fence, cross a meadow and on up the gentle incline of Randall Reid Mountain (so named for the black gentleman who homesteaded there). Here we found the hickory nut trees and, if the season favored, heavily laden huckleberry bushes (a wild form of blueberry).

Sometimes we would find a sweet gum tree and with a pocketknife borrowed from my brother, we would dig out the sticky gum I preferred to the fancy store-bought kind.

Our sacks now filled to overflowing, we would make our way to the bluffs for a brief rest. With our feet dangling over the edge, we would watch the train, far below, winding around the river on its way to Clarksville, and on to the state capital, Little Rock.

And we would dream our dreams.

Home again, the pecans and hickory nuts would be divided and put in a dry place until they could be cracked and the kernels put in a tight jar for their intended use.

Pecans, since they were plentiful, would go into salads, fudge and, of course, into greedy mouths. Hickory nuts, on the other hand, were saved for a special hickory nut cake. Black walnuts from a huge tree in our back yard were harvested for divinity. My father usually planted a few hills of peanuts for brittle, also popcorn. When the popcorn failed, we had a few ears of a certain kind of corn that made a palatable substitute.

Ingathering also included armloads of sumac, goldenrod and branches of red berries. Oh, yes, in the fall, my thoughts turn to those long ago ingatherings. And, here in my own back yard there is an ingathering too.

The late summer has brought a bounty of green tomatoes, enough for several jars of pickles and perhaps a green tomato mince pie or two for vegetarian friends.

I've salvaged enough grapes for a couple of quarts of juice and my basement is filled with the odor of drying herbs. I have gathered four-o'clock seeds to share with friends and there's plenty of garlic as a trade to a kind gentleman who brought me a sack of pine needles for my roses.

After being married and moving about the country for a number of years, I had forgotten the word "ingathering" until I went to work in the Society Department of The Wichita Eagle.

One fine fall day, Burt Doze, then managing editor of the evening Eagle, assigned me to cover a story about the Wichita Needlework Guild. "They're having an ingathering," he said.

Naturally I visualized an ingathering of food stuff. Not so. The Needlework Guild Ingathering was for clothing, lovely little dresses, suits and coats, sewn by members of the guild for needy children. Supplemented by store-bought shoes and other clothing necessities, these garments were distributed to children who might not have been able to attend school without them.

What impressed me most, each garment was one-of-a-kind, beautifully made. What joy they must have brought underprivileged children.

Through the years, while working in the media, it was my privilege to see this work continued. And, I am glad to say, the work still goes on. I tried to call the president, Mrs. Al Bissing, for an update on the ingathering. Perhaps she was at a meeting of the Guild. At any rate, it is gratifying to know that the word that afforded me so much pleasure as a child continues to bring comfort and happiness to other children today.

A LITTLE HUMBLE PIE

February 1984

I've come to the conclusion that none of us is ever completely in charge of his/her life. There's always the weather to remind us that there is a power greater than that of mind-over-matter mortals that can zap our best intentions, particularly the self-serving ones. Coping with weather can be a lesson in humility.

Last fall I decided to deal with snow by buying a front-wheel drive car. Since my garage was built for Model A Fords, my cars have had to live outside. With this car, I was determined to find a way to eliminate de-icing my windshields. Since a carport was out of the question until spring, I invested $65 in a nylon cover-all (I call it a shroud).

Something the salesman forgot to tell me — the car should be both clean and dry before shrouding. So I drove to the filling station where I trade only to learn that the car wash is closed for the winter. Back home I managed a fair cleaning job with warm water, sponge and plenty of drying cloths. Trying to get the shroud on in a stiff wind reminded me of the ridiculous antics I've seen in the movies. I expected any minute to be airborne. Finally the shroud was on and having a dry windshield was worth the effort. But what do you do when you come home after dark and it is snowing? You leave the car uncovered — right? That was the state of affairs in December when it snowed and snowed.

That is when I began to have twinges of humility. But I reminded myself that I was in charge, I had options. So I opted to stay indoors where it was warm.

Zap No. 2. One morning, after a nice sleep in a 68-degree temperature, I was awakened (about 6 a.m.) by my Sheltie, Charmaine, who was ready for her outside duties. As I reached for the bedside light, I noticed a frosty nip to the air. I turned the light switch, nothing happened. Burned-out bulb, I thought. I felt my way to the hallway switch — again nothing. Then I had a (pardon the pun) chilling thought, "the electricity is off."

Silly me. I felt my way back to the bedside table to get my glasses. Somehow glasses don't help a bit in the dark. Fortunately it was beginning to get a bit light (because it was snowing outside, I discovered), and I was able to find some matches and soon had three flames going in the middle of my dining room table. The thermostat read 60 degrees.

I let Charmaine out and watched from the window until she raced back to the warm (?) house. I got the newspaper off the front porch. With all that door fanning, the temp was now 52.

I called KG&E and, after being "on hold" for several minutes, a nice feminine voice took my report, sympathized with my plight and assured me that servicemen were on the job and doing everything possible to restore service.

I recalled that "layering" is the best way to conserve body heat. So, over my pajamas (and under my robe) went wool pants and turtleneck sweater; on my feet, fleece-lined boots; on my head, a cap; and on my hands, gloves.

There was plenty of hot water but have you ever tried to make instant coffee with tap water in a cold house? But even lukewarm,the coffee was comforting.

Libby, our cat (Charmaine owns him too) made a quick trip to the litter box in the basement before burrowing under the bedcovers. Charmaine, with her wool undercoat, was the warmest person (she thinks she's a people) in the house.

By now the snow was blotting out my neighbor's house, and I was beginning to feel isolated from the world. I called my friend Laura (thank goodness the telephone was in order) and she thought I should drive to her house. But that front-wheel drive didn't seem nearly so safe now. While I was lamenting I noticed a light from somewhere in the house — the electricity was back on and I was in charge again!

While I climbed out of all my wraps, I thanked the good Lord for putting such wonderful things as electricity and furnaces on Earth and for giving us service people who go out in all kinds of weather to maintain these services we take so for granted. Eating humble pie once in a while is good for all of us.

ALL NIGHT PERSONS

November 1984

Some folks welcome the end of daylight-saving time. Not me. I'm a night person. So I love the long daylight evenings and the late mornings. During the summer months, I get most of my yard work done after 6:30 or 7 p.m. And much of my indoor chores are done after that. This column is usually written after 10 p.m. and the "Barney Miller" show. By then the telephone has stopped ringing and I can stop running and enjoy these Moments with you.

My animals are night persons too. Should I go to bed before midnight my Sheltie, Charmaine, usually wakes me at about 2 a.m. to go out. She makes sure that no stray cat, opossum or coon has invaded her territory. Then she settles down on the back step to keep watch and count the stars.

Libby (Charmaine's cat) usually comes in for a midnight snack before settling down for what remains of the night. Libby sleeps around, so he may be on the foot of the bed, in his basket, or various other favorite spots.

Now that winter is coming on, both Charmaine and Libby are reluctant to come indoors at night. They sense that very soon they will be housebound with old you-know-who. Libby has the best of it. His windowsill perch allows him to sun himself on nice days and affords him a view of the neighborhood. Poor Charmaine must do with an occasional opening of the door and the short (on leash) walks around the block. When it snows, she loves to churn the back yard into an ugly mess.

But, when the wind blows, she must be taken out by force and she tries to beat me back through the door. As for old you-know-who, I'll miss my long Saturday walks. Actually, I don't mind winter too much as long as I don't have to be out in it; as long as the furnace keeps the house warm; the power doesn't go off; as long as I can pay my utility bills and the telephone keeps me linked to the outside world. And, of course, as long as I have plenty of reading material, popcorn and apples.

November brings an end to the yearlong political debate. I doubt that many of us will be 100 percent satisfied with the outcome. But then, when were we ever 100 percent happy with anything? We Americans have the unique privilege of saying whatever we please about our officeholders. When I get too upset with broken campaign promises and excuses, I try to remind myself of the story of the man whose sons were always bickering. He demonstrated how easily sticks can be broken, one by one, and how it is almost impossible to break them when bundled together, therefore proving that "united we stand, divided we fall."

Now that winter is coming on, let's exchange some "remember whens." I'll start. Remember when, in the days before hairsprays, we would boil flax seed and strain the goo into a jar to set our hair? It worked especially well on finger waves and spit curls.

A CLEAN UNBLOTTED PAGE

January 1985

Thirty years ago, on radio station KFBI (now KFDI) I broadcast a program for New Year's Day. Many people liked the program and asked me to repeat it. Today, as I reread that script I realize that I have many of the same feelings I had when I first presented the program. So, with your indulgence, and in a much shorter version, I present it in updated form as my New Year's Moments:

"As I write this, the first day of January, 1985, is still a white, unblotted page of the future, that in a short time will have been blurred with mistakes, broken resolutions and tragedy — all the unforeseen catastrophes of January, 1985.

"But, for now, the page is spotless, reminding me of how, as a child, I used to thrill at the sight of a new school tablet, its pages unblemished by mistakes, and how hard I tried to keep that first page perfect, believing that to do so would ensure perfection throughout all the other pages. And, when I did smudge the paper, I would tear it out and start on another, only to have the same thing happen again. At last, I would give up striving for perfection and the tablet, just like all the others, would be full of crossed-out beginnings and blotted errors.

"I always hoped that someday I would be able to write so carefully, so accurately and so beautifully, that my entire tablet would be something to admire, to be held up before the entire class as a shining example.

"Needless to say, that miracle never came about, just as it never came about that a year was perfect — free from all mistakes, heartaches and blunders.

"I know, at last, that there will never be a year, or even a day, when everything will be exactly right — flawless. When such perfection is reached, time probably will not be measured at all.

"But, for now, New Year's Day is a white spotless page. It is beautiful, yes, but would we want to keep it that way, even if we could? Would we know how to live every hour, minute, second, surrounded by perfection? What inspiration could a minister have for his sermons if the members of his congregation sat under halos? How could a poet write of joy if he had never known sorrow?

How could an artist catch the glory of twilight if there were no shadows? How could a little child's smile be so sweet if there were never tears nor tantrums with which to compare? What possible attraction could heaven have if suddenly Earth and all upon it became perfect?

"It seems that most of us are composed of both good and bad. In some the bad overbalances the good, and we have our criminals, corrupt politicians, dictators and traitors. When the good overbalances the bad, we have our finest doctors, nurses, teachers and benefactors. But most of us are so equally balanced in good and bad that our lives are paradoxical. We are unable to predict our reactions to certain situations, temptations and impulses. Just when we want to be our best, the bad will crop out. And, when we least expect it, we find the courage to face overwhelming obstacles.

"Today I look regretfully backwards on 1984 and, like Janus the two-headed god for which January is named, look hopefully forward to 1985. My regrets are mainly for sins of omission, all the good intentions that got sidetracked somewhere along the span of 365 days. I regret the neglect of good friends, the little notes of condolences, the words of sympathy and understanding that might have lightened their burdens.

"I remember with guilt the many things done in my behalf by friends who were not properly thanked, the forgotten birthdays and anniversaries of many who are dear to me. These omissions seem small individually but, at year's end, they stack to an alarming height, particularly when I try to balance them with the accomplishments of the years. I hope that in 1985 I shall become a better manager of my time so that I may do the little things for others that will help make their lives worthwhile."

This is a very shortened version of the 30-year-old broadcast, when I was much younger. I'm afraid I haven't improved as much in those 30 years as I had hoped for. But I'm still working on it.

And, as I look back over those 30 years I realize how very lucky I am to have known and grown older with so many of you who now read Active Aging. And, while life hasn't been perfect or without unhappy times, it has been interesting and more rewarding than I deserve. My wish for all of you in this coming year is good friends, good health and, most of all, LOVE.

GUESS WHO CAME TO DINNER

July 1985

Don't you hate people who say, "I've got some good news and some bad news — first the good news" and the good news never measures up to the bad news? Well I'll tell you my bad stuff first. You may not want to wait around for the good.

It began when an opossum came to dinner and stayed for a week. In fact he/she/it might have been in my basement longer than that. I keep cat food on a table on the enclosed back porch for Libby, my liberated tomcat who likes to snack whenever he pleases. For several nights I thought I heard something eating his food and decided it was a mouse.

My basement stairs are reached by lifting a trapdoor in a pantry off my back porch. I usually leave it open so Libby can go down and visit with the mice (he's too well-fed to bother catching them).

One night I heard ominous sounds in the pantry. I flipped on the light and there, sitting among the canned goods on the shelf was this young opossum.

I closed the door to my kitchen and a window to prevent his moving into the house, then I proceeded to direct him out the back door. The opossum opted to hide on the porch. I moved everything out there, trying to find him. No luck. Exhausted, I went to bed. About 2 a.m. I heard a noise, turned on the light and there on the window ledge (right back of my bed) sat the opossum blinking at me through the window.

This went on for six nights and seven days when, just short of a nervous breakdown, I caught the little freeloader in a trap. The nice folks at the animal shelter took him to some wooded area where he will probably find a mate, raise a family and bring them all back to eat Libby's food.

•••••

That's the way things started the week of my 75th birthday. On that day, after a sumptuous brunch and fun get-together with friends, I returned home relaxed and content. But not for long.

The tree trimmers provided by a utility company had mutilated my beautiful hackberry tree (damaging my fence for good measure). The tree didn't look so bad from my side of the fence (except for the loss of a limb that had shaded the back porch) but, from the alley, my tree looked like a top heavy pregnant woman about to topple over from her own weight. Every limb on the east side had been amputated. I was too mad to cry.

I can't believe the utility company wanted this slaughter of our beautiful trees. The whole neighborhood is upset. To make matters worse, two of our neighbors are in the hospital, one from a stroke and one from a bad fall that injured his hip. And, on the day after my birthday, I almost never made it to Sunday School. A man barreled out of his driveway missing me by inches. Rather I missed him. My reflexes at 75 are still pretty good. I managed to swerve enough to miss the backing car, a parked car on the right and a parked truck on the left, thus avoiding damage except to my nerves. I just hope it scared him as much as it scared me.

Are you still with me? When my editor sees this she may decide not to inflict my "gloom and doom" Moments on you. Come to think about it, with the kind of luck I've had with the mail service lately, this column may never reach her. But that's enough bad news for now.

•••••

The good news? Well, for me, the best news is "to be alive" at 75. And, considering the events of the past two weeks, I've learned some things that helped offset the bad.

The nice lady at the animal shelter advised me that mothballs spread on the basement floor would discourage opossum visitation. Maybe that advice will help others who have opossum problems.

WORDS FOR ERNIE'S BOSS

August 1985

I hope Ernie's boss reads this. Ernie works as a stock clerk at a discount store, the one that recently changed its name. In case his boss is interested, Ernie saved him a customer — namely me.

I saw the store's ad for an outdoor cooker at an attractive sale price. "Just the thing to tide me over until I make up my mind about a new stove," I thought. There were several other sale items I was interested in but it was the cooker that got me out of the cool air-conditioned house, into my hot car and to the store.

Once inside I didn't see any cookers so I wandered around until I saw a clerk and asked her where to find one. I could tell right away I hadn't made her day. She stomped around several aisles before stopping and pointing "up there" and then stomped away.

"Up there" was the top shelf about a foot and a half above my head. By standing on tiptoe and stretching my arm, I could just touch the top of the shelf. A young man with a clipboard came into view, and I asked him if he would get one of the smokers down for me.

I hadn't made his day either. Without a word he lifted one of the cookers (in a box) down, placed it on the floor and said, "Open it and check it out before you buy it," and walked away.

The box, about 2 feet square and 3 feet deep, was held together by big staples. My first reaction was to walk away but, I thought, that was too easy. Somehow I was going to open that box, empty everything on the floor THEN leave — leave the store — forever.

Opening the box wasn't too difficult, getting everything out wasn't too easy. Everything was fitted in so tightly that all I got out was the lid.

I was aware that another clerk was at the end of the aisle stocking shelves. I commented, loudly enough for him to hear, "They would sell more of these cookers if they would at least put one together so a customer could see what they look like."

In about three seconds the clerk was standing before me. He was scarcely taller than I and had one of the friendliest faces I've ever looked into. He smiled and said, "Do you know that I started putting these smokers together and they sold so fast we had to re-order and I had to stop because I wasn't getting anything else done."

He then took everything out of the box and, although he didn't put it together, he explained how to do it and assured me it was very easy. I learned that he had worked in a retirement hotel and that he had enjoyed the residents there. "I learned from them how to be patient. Those folks were just great."

While he put everything back into the box, I learned a great deal more about the young man. I told him, "I hope your boss appreciates you and gives you a promotion." He beamed, "Oh, I hope so too."

After he had put the box in my cart he said, "If you need any help, I'll be glad to take it to your car. Just ask for Ernie." He had put me in such a good mood, I went ahead and bought several more bargains. No, I didn't ask for Ernie to help me get the cooker into my car trunk. When I got to the check-out counter, I heard one of the clerks complaining about a problem.

"Get Ernie," the cashier said. "He'll fix it for you." If I have any problem putting the cooker together I know where to get help.

HOT HEAD, COOL COLUMN

December 1985

Because I am such a disorganized person, Marie's Moments often get written piecemeal, on the run and in various places. This column, for instance, has its beginning under the dryer at the beauty salon. It's not easy to write a cool column with a hot head. I try to remember all the wonderful ideas I had but they have evaporated in this bonnet that fits around my ears. So I find myself looking out into the booths of the salon hoping to see something that will spark an idea into my cooking brain.

And what do I see? In one booth a hairdresser is working (it's called styling) the hair of a young man in his 20s. Down the line another male is getting a trim, and over there — is he? Yes, he is — he's getting a permanent.

I understand that in some of the really "posh" salons (this one is medium posh) the male yuppies go regularly to have their hair streaked, their mustaches trimmed and their eyebrows tweaked.

Back during the '20s, I used to have my hair cut (Flapper Fanny style) in the barbershop. So, I'm used to seeing men being shaved (and dusted with lots of talcum powder), getting their hair cut, their shoes shined and on rare occasions, their nails manicured.

There weren't many so-called beauty shops in those days and, if there had been, a man wouldn't have been caught dead in one.

But then, in those days women didn't wear hard hats, jeans and mechanic's overalls. World War II, with the arrival of Rosie the Riveter, changed all that.

Women soon learned that slacks were a lot more comfortable, practical and safer, than skirts for their new war-working roles. They no longer had to worry about their skirts while boarding crowded buses, or keeping their legs modestly crossed at the ankles while seated. And everyone knows that putting your feet up can be beneficial after a hard day's work. Pants made that possible.

Changing lifestyles always affect our manner of dress. Back in the heyday of kings and queens, men were very style conscious — powdered wigs, buckled shoes, colorful coats and breeches, jewelry and snuff boxes. And women, bless our little hearts, always have had the capacity to fit the dress to the role, whether it be wife, mother, club woman or volunteer or someone doing all of these while taking another step up the corporate ladder. She might wear a hard hat and jeans during the day then emerge with upswept hair, multicolored eye shadow, low-cut cocktail dress and 5-inch heels for an evening on the town.

And, I have to admit, I like the well-groomed man with his professionally styled hair and trimmed beard much better than the long, straggly, unkempt look of a few years ago.

Time to get out from under the dryer and on to other subjects.

FAREWELL TO THE GRAPES

October 1985

Well, folks, I finally did it. I cut down my grapevines. At least I've cut down the Concords that have been holding up my garage for the past 30 years, and I've started on the ones that have been climbing over my garden fence.

I've been threatening to cut them down ever since the little black-eyed bandits (raccoons) joined the birds in robbing the vines of fruit. I didn't mind the birds pigging out on my grapes, they earn their keep in slowing down the bug population and by being a beautiful part of nature. But the coons wore out their welcome when they ganged up on my Sheltie, Charmaine, and gave her a bloody nose.

I had already decided that this would be the year I would actually cut down the grapes. I planned to wait until they put out those long, lovely new branches that could be shaped in wreaths, but before I could get-a-round-tuit those branches were full of grapes. Oh, well, I decided to wait yet another year.

Then one morning, while one of the squirrels was

putting on a show for Charmaine, it happened. The little bushy-tail was doing acrobatics, swinging from limb to limb, chattering up a storm. Charmaine was barking her applause so loudly I almost didn't hear the noise that scared the poor little squirrel so badly it slid down a branch and fell onto the roof of the garage. I thought the tree branch had broken but it snapped back into the air.

Puzzled, I started back into the house, then I saw what had happened. The large branch of the Concord over the garage door had broken from its own weight.

My first impulse was to drag the vine to the alley and let the birds and coons take over. Somehow I just couldn't do it. I picked some of the best bunches for a neighbor who loves grapes. Then I got a basket and started harvesting the clusters of fruit (both ripe and green). Then I filled a 5-gallon pail and a plastic dishpan. It was as if the grapevine was determined to produce enough fruit to last me the years after it had been cut down. And if that fruit had ripened, the yield would have been overwhelming.

I do not enjoy making jelly but how could I ignore the efforts of my faithful old grapevine? Unlike other years when I had miserable luck getting the stuff to jell, this batch was almost good.

So the Concord is down and the others will follow. Now all I have to do is find a place to store the vines until I get around to making those wreaths. Oh, yes. Now I will have to have a new garage since the vines are not there to support the old one.

BABY: IN FROM THE COLD

March 1986

As I share my Moments today, it is snowing and the 15-above-zero seems bitterly cold after the 60-plus of just a few days ago.

So, those of us associated with Old Cowtown Museum and the Empire House restaurant are thankful to know that Baby is out of the cold.

The story of Baby lacks a proper beginning. I first became aware of her one cold fall day two or three years ago. As I parked my car at Cowtown I glimpsed a young dachshund crouched among the native grasses on the berm that separates the commercial area of Cowtown from the parking area.

I spent several minutes trying to coax her to me, but when I moved toward her she ran away. No one at Cowtown knew when or where the dog had come from. No one came to claim her. Winter was coming, and we worried about her being out in the cold. There were those who would have adopted her, but she seemed unable to trust anyone enough to let them approach her.

Folks at the Empire House made sure that the little dog had food and water. She evidently found enough shelter under the boardwalks along with the Cowtown cats to survive the winters. One of the chefs at the Empire House was able to observe that the little dog had been mistreated and probably had been abandoned at the Cowtown grounds (or perhaps had run away to escape further punishment).

That part of her life we will never know.

Time went on. People continued to try to make

friends with the little dog and she seemed to want to make friends but was still unable to trust us.

Nancy and John Avery, who own the Victorian-style photograph gallery in Cowtown, continued their daily efforts to make friends with the dog. Since the word "baby" was used so often in the coaxing, the little dog began to respond to the word and, so it seemed natural to call her Baby. And at last, Baby began to trust the Cowtown folks. One day she followed Nancy into the gallery and when Nancy sat down, she jumped into her lap. Once that contact was made she couldn't seem to get enough of human attention.

Most of all, she trusted the folks who seemed to be a permanent part of Cowtown, particularly those who fed her. So one day the chef at the Empire House invited Baby to be a part of his home. Baby accepted and, at last report, is showing her appreciation by shaking hands, rolling over and performing other tricks she had learned sometime long ago.

I'm so glad Baby now has a home, that she has learned that there are kind humans. But, Baby, I'm going to miss you.

GOODBYE, OLD GARAGE

September 1986

> *If all the world was apple pie*
> *And all the sea was ink;*
> *If all the trees were bread and cheese*
> *What would we have to drink?*

Perhaps some of you remember that little poem. It was in my first-grade primer (we called them readers) and its composer never knew what fears he instilled into my young mind.

Every time our well was low, I worried, "What will we have to drink?" Years later, during the drouth in South Dakota (when there was no water for animals, and water for humans was brought in by train) that little worry niggled at the corner of my memory. "What will we have to drink?"

A recent tour of the Wichita Water Treatment Plant once again brought that little poem to mind. The plant is less than a block from my home and I've always wondered just what went on behind that brick wall. So I welcomed the chance to observe, firsthand, what steps are taken from the time the water arrives from its sources until it is channeled out to homes, factories and business places in Wichita.

It was such an interesting and enlightening tour. Our guide, Jeff White, is a chemist whose job it is to test the water, monitor any changes and make sure the finished product comes to our taps palatable and potable.

Seeing the water in its original state, murky and sinister looking; watching it travel through the different filtering and purifying tanks until the final stages when it is crystal clear, did a lot to make me more appreciative of the chemists, engineers and technology that make the best-of-all-drinks even better.

There seems to be plenty of God-given water for our area, but when I stood before the little meter that ticks off the gallons of water being used and saw the millions of gallons that had already been used, I recalled that ominous little line, "What would we have to drink?"

Thanks to our water department and the Giver of all good gifts, I hope I'll never be faced with that problem.

But I came away determined to be a bit more saving of the water we take for granted.

•••••

My Moments today are full of nostalgia. A little one-car garage that has been part of my life for more than 30 years is being torn down (in fact, as I wrote those words, the roof caved in). It was built in the days of Model A Fords and other narrow, top heavy autos.

When my husband and I moved into our little Riverside cottage, it was with the expectation that our vintage Dodge would also, at long last, have a home. But it was not to be.

Driving through the narrow doors without scraping the sides of the car was difficult. Backing out was nigh impossible. So once again the Dodge (and the other cars that followed) had to endure the seasons in the driveway.

The garage became a workshop for my husband's many projects, storage for the lawnmower and gardening equipment and catchall for various accumulations: campaign signs, old car tags, cigar boxes filled with nuts, bolts, screws, hinges, et cetera. Glass jars were filled with nails, old saws hung on the walls. A loft that could be raised and lowered became a storeroom for screens, doors, boxes, etc.

When my sister came to live with us, she brought along a truckload of accumulated "treasures." What couldn't be housed was garaged. When friends needed a place to store a gas range, it became a permanent addition to rust away through the years. Now the garden and the back yard are filled with all these things that had to be put somewhere until the new garage is built. The new building will have an additional 5 by 12 feet of space to accommodate some of the stuff — but not all. So now it is a matter of what goes and what stays.

The two young men (one a teenager) who moved the stuff commented that it was like "walking into the past." Indeed it is. In the garden is the old (really old) treadle Singer, reminding me that before I was born my mother made clothes for my sisters on that machine. Nearby is a round-topped trunk that might have accompanied my father from Georgia to Arkansas more than a hundred years ago. There is a horseshoe my husband placed over the side door of the garage for good luck. I don't know that it ever brought good luck, but at least it never fell on anyone's head.

I'm sure that the demise of the old garage will deprive the various cats, opossums, birds and other wildlife that found refuge there. I hope the new one will be animal-proof.

Goodbye little garage. You deserve a better fate.

FOR THOSE CHILBLAINS

February 1987

When our first big snow was predicted last month, it reminded me that the feeder must be cleaned and filled for the cardinals, juncos and other birds that winter here.

During the mild weather, the birds and squirrels found plenty of food but once the ground is covered with snow, the seed pods left from last summer's flowers and the pecans and walnuts are hidden, and the little creatures trust their human friends to provide them sustenance until spring.

As much as I love birds and animals, it is during the

winter months I appreciate them most. My bird feeder was made by Ralph Brooks who creates them, along with other beautiful wooden items, each year for our church bazaar. It has a glass window that helps portion the bird-seed. I place the feeder on a fence opposite my kitchen window where I can watch the activity while washing dishes or peeling potatoes.

The larger birds are apt to crowd out the little fellows in their rush to get at the sunflower seeds. But in doing so, they scatter the tinier seeds to the ground below where the smaller ones can get their fill.

I try to keep the patch of ground clear for that purpose. Once in a while a squirrel will try to get a handout but the birds usually flog him away. Last winter a big black bird put on a show that was funnier than any comedy I've seen on the TV screen. He was too big to perch on the tiny porch so he tried sitting on top but then he couldn't reach the feed. Once he managed to hang upside down but then he had his back to the feeder. He tried hanging to the fence with one foot while holding onto the feed with the other. That only served to push the feeder farther away, causing Mr. Blackbird to do an ungraceful split before falling to the ground.

I almost felt sorry for the bird, watching his frustration. Over and over he tried to reach the food while the cardinals and other birds waited patiently in the nearby lilac bush for him to give up.

Finally, with an exasperated "caw" he flew away, reminding me of Edgar A. Poe's "The Raven," with his melancholy, "Nevermore."

The sycamore tree in my back yard with the leaves gone, is a showcase for a winter circus. Squirrels are the performers — the acrobats, highwire walkers and trapeze artists. There are two pairs nesting in the tree and their antics rival any monkey shenanigans I've ever seen under the big top.

They chase one another up and down the tree trunk, fly from one limb to another. Then they race each other on the electric cable, somersaulting in the air back to the tree.

When Charmaine, my Sheltie, gets cabin fever during the winter, I let her out to act as ringmaster for the squirrels. She dances around on her hind legs, barking frantically. Soon Susy, my neighbor's black cocker and Heidi, Marsha's dachshund from across the alley, join in the commotion. Their tails fanning the breeze are as much an indication of enjoyment as any human applause. Who says animals are dumb?

The Canada geese have returned. They seem to consider Wichita their winter headquarters. Most years I have had to drive to the 11th Street bridge to see them but now my house has become part of the flight pattern for a small number that fly over about 4 p.m. each day. This is about the time I take Charmaine for her walk around the block. The first time she heard their honking she stopped and looked around to discover the source of the noise. Now she accepts them as a part of her afternoon entertainment and barks companionably.

•••••

Does anyone out there know a remedy for chilblains? Some 40 years ago during a blizzard, my feet became badly frostbitten. Since then, especially during winter, I have had to get up during the night to bathe my feet in cold water to stop the misery. So if you know something that will help … PLEASE let me know.

•••••

March 1987

Speaking of blizzards, you may recall that last
month I asked for suggestions to relieve my chilblains
that have been bothering me since my feet were frostbitten in a Minnesota blizzard years ago.

The response has been tremendous. I've gotten so
many suggestions I don't know which to try first. Some
of the good folks asked that their names not be used so,
to make sure I don't violate someone's request, I will
omit all names. But I want each of you to know how
grateful I am to you for taking time to call and write.
Several of you have had chilblains and have shared with
me the remedies that gave you relief. Others have copied
down remedies you have heard or read about.

One writer who has suffered from a frostbitten toe
for more than 50 years called to share a remedy given to
her by the driver of a Foster Grandparent van (you
guessed it, she's a Foster Grandparent).

He told her to soak cotton in pure alcohol and tape
it around the toe for the night. She got almost instant
relief. Since I have some alcohol on hand I'm going to try
it first.

A book, "The Farm and Household Cyclopedia,"
printed at least 100 years ago, offers some fascinating
remedies. One was to sprinkle slices of raw, unpeeled
potatoes with salt, then drain off the liquid and bathe the
chilblains in it. Only one application is necessary, the
book says.

Another (unfailing) remedy calls for a solution of 30
grains of permanganate of potassium in an ounce of pure
water to be applied with a brush or as a poultice. The only
definition I could find for permanganate described it as a

dark purple crystalline compound, and potassium as a metallic element of the alkali metal group. I decided against it. I might get purple feet that glow in the dark.

Several remedies mentioned coal oil, turpentine and snow. One nice lady even gave me the name of her doctor and the ingredients he prescribed for her chilblains. My own doctor suggested a similar, over-the-counter treatment. With all these great suggestions I'm bound to get relief. I'll try to keep you posted. Meantime, thanks, thanks, thanks.

ADVICE FOR PACKRATS

July 1981

I've got to get my house in order. Oh, no, I'm not expecting to take my leave for at least 10 years, but at the rate I'm going it's going to take me that long to clear out the accumulations of almost 30 years in my five-room cottage.

Before moving to Wichita, my husband and I had been on the move, living out of a suitcase, so to speak. We had a small apartment here for a time. Then, joy of joys, we found this little house with a yard, trees, great neighbors — our first and only house! We shared and loved it for 15 years and, during that time, made up for all those years when we had to limit our belongings to those things we could haul in the back of our car.

During 15 years of widowhood, I've continued the pack rat movement, collecting books, tools, dishes, et cetera. My car automatically pulls up to the curb where there is a "garage sale" sign.

Now I'm beginning to feel like one of those recluses

in the book "My Brother's Keeper," in which two brothers completely fill their house with things until they had to follow strings in order to find their way in and out on their infrequent trips to buy food. One brother died, and the accumulation finally tumbled down and smothered the other one. The nightmare I had after reading that book started me thinking, "that could happen to me."

Then, for the past two weeks, I've watched a friend of mine trying to deal with the frustration of ridding a 10-room house (plus attic and basement) of beautiful old furniture, dishes, clothing and paintings that had belonged to a beloved aunt. Seeing strangers pawing through the personal belongings of a person she had loved, carelessly spilling ashes on the floor, constantly asking, "Will you take less for this?" left her exhausted and depressed.

I don't want that burden on the shoulders of my stepdaughters. So I'm gritting my teeth and trying, at least, to get rid of the surplus. After all, who needs dozens of glass insulators, 30 mayonnaise jars, thousands of Christmas cards and all those milk cartons my husband saved to plant things in. Wish me luck.

•••••

September 1981

My July column brought a sympathetic response from several readers who, like myself, have accumulations of "stuff" overrunning their attics, basements and garages. And they want to know how I am going about bringing order to chaos.

Well, I haven't gotten as far as I would like but I do have a plan that I will share with you. I'll take you as far as I've gone and next month I'll bring you another progress report. If your accumulation is as large as mine, it will take you several days to take care of the preliminaries.

My brother used to say, "Always plan your work then work your plan ... and keep it simple." So here goes. First, be sure you have cleared a space to work in. Have handy several trash bags (heavy duty is best), large and small paper sacks (or wrapping paper), string and boxes of all sizes. You also will need marking pencils.

Now sort your accumulation into three categories: 1. To keep. 2. To discard. 3. To sell or give away. In your to-keep pile, go all of those canceled checks, receipts and everything pertaining to your back taxes. Put them all in a sack or box and mark it plainly for sorting later. In another sack, ditto for old policies, warranties, proofs of purchase papers and the like. In still another, all letters, greeting cards, mementos and the like. Also, in this pile put clothing, books, pictures and all other items you can't part with.

As you sort, put all discards in the trash bags. As you fill them, carry them to the trash cans. That way you will have more room in which to work, and you won't be so apt to change your mind and put things back in the to-keep pile.

Into the third pile go the books, clothing, furniture and what-nots you don't need, don't have room for and yet consider too good to throw away.

Well, space is going fast. Between now and next month sort over all those tax papers. To be on the safe side, you had best keep everything that pertains to your taxes for the past five years. Dispose of the rest (I tear all personal papers up before sending them to the trash can). In five large envelopes (sacks will do), put each year's collection, tie them into a neat package and on the outside write "tax papers for (year)." Put these into a box or sack, tie securely and label. Now when you have paid your taxes (income, property and personal) for this year, follow this same procedure. Keep in a safe place for several months then place with the other envelopes and destroy the oldest ones. For example, when you add the 1981 receipts, destroy those for 1976.

If you have some time left before our next visit, use it to sort over all those magazines, books and recipes. Next month I'll give you some suggestions for the disposal of those "to sell or give away items."

•••••

October 1981

I promised to continue some suggestions for clearing your home of those accumulations that threaten to close in on you, specifically some suggestions for disposing of those "to sell or give away items."

There comes a time when we just have to admit we made some bad buys in clothing. Clothes that were becoming when we were younger (thinner, trimmer), now seem to accent our wrinkles and worst figure faults. Shoes that fit in the store crucify our feet on the street. Sweaters we love but can't wear because they itch and give us a rash.

Stop giving those dogs space. If they are in good condition and in style, you may be able to get something back on your investment. First air them out, brush and press them.

Now consider:

• Calling some friends in for coffee and displaying the items at a moderate fee. Or perhaps you could invite them to bring their own misfits and have an exchange party.

• Taking them to a resale shop where the owner retains a certain percentage of the resale fee. It won't be great but it will put the burden on someone else's shoulders.

• If they don't sell and none of your friends or relatives want them for free, the Salvation Army, church-owned resale shops and veterans' shops welcome clothing, particularly serviceable clothing in good repair.

• Are some of the items old enough to fit in the "nostalgia" category? Many resale shops put a good price tag on old-fashioned petticoats, pantaloons, bloomers, shawls, beaded bags, combs and fans. These are also sought by museums.

The clothing of the 1940s and '50s appeal to many young people who like "campy" clothes. Stiletto-heeled shoes are worn by the disco set.

Theatrical groups also look for dated clothes. While you won't be able to sell your clothing to museums and non-profit shops, you have the right to ask for a signed paper listing your donations. It will list the approximate dollar value on a blank space for you to fill in. This can give you a substantial tax write-off.

•••••

November 1981

I promised one of our readers some suggestions for disposing of the clothing and personal effects belonging to her late husband. She has been unable to dispose of them in conventional ways (yard sales, flea markets, etc). "I couldn't bear to see people paw over them and haggle over prices," she wrote.

I know the feeling, having gone through the same

trauma. Clothing that has been worn by a loved one is a particular problem. I remember packing all my husband's clothing for Operation Holiday only to unpack his better suits and top coat. I couldn't bear the thought of their being given to someone who might sell them for drugs or wine.

I sent all the warm clothing that would be appreciated by a needy person. Then, as a last resort, I sold the better clothing at a garage sale to a young man just starting a new job. I lowered the price to $50 then made the mistake of accepting a check that took me three days to collect. The stress was offset by sending the money to a step-grandson who was struggling through college — a gift from his grandfather.

If money is no consideration (and she says it isn't) our reader might check with some of the churches to see if they have a list of needy and deserving persons. Some churches, such as the Mennonites, have a year-round program of distributing clothing and bedding to the needy and disaster victims.

I found that my husband's fishing buddies were pleased to take over his fishing gear and some of the younger chess players were happy to have the chess set and books. My stepdaughters took his jewelry (cuff links, tie tacs and the like) to their husbands. And the men in the canasta club each chose a tie. Somehow it was comforting to have them wear the ties at our get-togethers and just talking about some of the good times we had all had made my life less lonely.

Our reader wishes there existed "a common outlet where others like me could take these articles, knowing they would be handled with consideration … where I could bring myself to let go without anguish." I hope some of you may know of such a place.

•••••

December 1981

When I started writing the "cleaning out" series months ago, I felt duty bound to follow my own advice. So the trash haulers have really earned their money collecting the stuff that has been overflowing my basement and garage.

As a matter of fact those collections just may be giving me the reputation as a lush. Several years ago, I became fascinated with the wine bottle candles that were being used in an Italian restaurant.

You know, the kind where you burn colored candles and let the wax run down the sides in waterfall fashion. I must have planned to go in the candle business because I collected wine, beer and whiskey bottles (at garage sales) and had about 30 of them that went into the trash barrel. I hope trash haulers are not gossips.

While I didn't accomplish everything I planned, I'm happy to report I now have room enough in my basement that I don't trip over things when I need to clean the furnace filter. And there is actually room enough in my garage for the lawnmower and gardening tools (not my car though; my garage was built for the narrow but tall Model Ts).

Of course there are still several boxes for disposal. Old papers and letters to be sorted this winter (the stamps will be saved for collectors); books for the Art Museum Book Fair; magazines for nursing homes; and a box of cosmetics, notepaper, decks of cards and the like that I hope the women at the Crisis Center can use.

But what does one do with a 14-year collection of dog toys (rawhide sticks, a squeaky mouse, etc.) that belonged to two beloved Shelties who have gone to pet heaven?

Since our last visit I've had two great suggestions for the reader who didn't want to sell her husband's things at a garage sale and wanted to be sure they would go to a deserving and appreciative person.

My next-door neighbor suggested the veterans hospital. "That's where I sent my husband's good clothing. There are lots of men there who need and appreciate them."

A reader, who signs herself "a retired friend," shared an experience she had when her 92-year-old mother died, leaving some lovely clothing. Being a member of the Eastern Star, this reader was aware that many women and men living in the Masonic Home have no families and no way of replenishing their wardrobes. Later she was rewarded by seeing a dear elderly lady wearing an entire outfit that had belonged to her mother. What great ideas! I do hope they will help others with their problems.

This is the last of the "advice to pack rats" series. I hope it helped others who have the "never throw anything away" syndrome. But time to move on.

•••••

January 1990

It's 1990, folks. Time to shut the door on the old year, time to look ahead to a new decade. At least it will be by the time you read this. But, as I write these Moments, it is still 1989 and I'm still trying to tie up the loose ends of THIS decade.

As a matter of fact, just today, I finally completed (almost) a project that began nine years ago when I first started writing this column.

Some of you may recall those first columns dealt with "ways to reduce excess clutter" in your attics, garages and/or basements. The idea being, as I gave you the methods I was to be using those same methods to clear out a 10-year accumulation of letters from my husband's office, boxes of scripts from years of broadcasting at the old KFBI station and 11 years of files and tearsheets of my work at The Eagle and Beacon.

I hope the methods worked faster for you than they did for me. I managed to get the office and radio stuff cleared out but all the other accumulation, along with boxes of tax receipts, Christmas cards, research papers and magazines filled up the vacant spots.

Which just goes to prove something I've suspected all along: Plans work better on paper than they do in implementation.

The plans were: Throw out everything that isn't needed or doesn't have value. How do you place need and value on boxes of letters from children, family members and friends? How do you dispose of magazines that might have your favorite recipe somewhere within their pages? And when might you need some of those receipts to prove that you "did too" pay your taxes on time?

One evening I went through letters from my stepchildren (my husband had carefully filed them according to date — 1957 to 1962). Those were the years they were getting married and having children (children now with children of their own). Each letter brought so many memories — the year Molly and family went to Germany — when Barbara almost died of polio — when Dee's children started to school. I laughed and cried as I tore each one up and put them into paper sacks.

I spent hours getting the excess into one area of the basement. Then I paid an out-of-work man to haul it all away. I wanted him to take the stuff to a recycling place but he said it wouldn't pay enough to be worth the time or trip.

Now I can walk around my basement without having to move boxes to make a path. Oh, there is still some excess (the stack of Active Aging is getting pretty high). But, in the new year, I'm going to try very hard to cut down on the clutter: newspapers to the vet, bottles to recycling areas, magazines to care homes and the beauty salon, and books to the book fairs.

This isn't the type of New Year's Moments I had planned to write — no, it was going to be one of those inspirational, lofty types. But, somehow it seemed important to let you know that, at long last, I have completed some of those plans that I outlined for you nine years ago.

ENJOYING NATURE

July 1987

Cool thoughts for a hot summer day: Not everyone enjoys, as I do, the native grasses planted on the berms that circle the west and southwest borders of Old Cowtown Museum. History buffs appreciate the fact that these grasses and, yes, some weeds, are the same plants that existed on the prairie before it was turned into farmland.

But even those folks who ask, "Why don't you mow those weeds?" surely would enjoy the berms today. In addition to the natural grasses, there are hundreds of native wildflowers. Such a display must have lightened the heart of many a homesick newcomer to Kansas back

54

in the 1870s.

There are the delicate pinks of the thistle poppy and mallows, the blues of cornflowers and the rich yellow, gold and red flowers with the dark cone centers (names I have forgotten). What fun pioneer children must have had gathering colorful bouquets for their mothers. If you have always thought of sunflowers as the only native wildflower in Kansas, do please drive over to Cowtown and enjoy your surprise.

•••••

Just next door to the frontier beauty of Cowtown is the newly opened Botanica. Those of you who attended the grand opening surely will long remember the thousands of gorgeous roses in black containers. They were breathtaking, as were the blossoms in the outdoor pool.

There was plenty of outdoor entertainment, including the senior tap dancers, Tap Katz. They looked mighty spiffy in their white shirts and pants, red bow ties and straw hats, and they did some fancy footwork.

•••••

Last year, two robins built their nest in my neighbor's snowball bush next to the fence just outside my kitchen window. I enjoyed watching the industrious pair as they gathered materials for their nest and prepared for their family. Then one bright morning there were three pairs of beaks poked above the nest, and the parents were kept busy feeding their hungry babies.

One morning I heard the furious calling of birds and knew that the babies were learning to fly and that a cat was stalking them. I rushed to the rescue and managed to catch the cat as it lunged for the frightened baby.

A day or so after, I heard the robins' anguished cries

and rushed out to see a neighbor's cat with one of the birds in its mouth. I mourned with the parents but was relieved that it hadn't been my Libby that caught the little one. I love cats but I hate their bird-killing instinct.

This year, the robins must have considered the snowball bush enemy territory. I miss them so and I envy my neighbors, Phil and Roslyn Hoch. Two beautiful swallows have chosen the eaves of their porch for a nest. Birds are a wonderful compensation for not owning a cat.

THE RUSH TO RUDENESS

January 1988

I stopped making New Year's resolutions a number of years ago, but I'm about to make one for 1988 — to slow down and make each day count.

I've just come from a wonderful concert presented by the Wichita Symphony and Friends University Singing Quakers. It was the type of concert you would expect to pay from $4 to $15 to hear. The only admission charge was an item of food for the food bank, and that wasn't mandatory.

There was a jam-packed audience for the program in Convention Hall of Century II. The applause indicated an appreciative audience. Even so, during the last number, many people began hurrying down the steps to the exit.

I'm sure it wasn't their intention to be rude to the musicians and singers or to the rest of us who were trying to hear the final number. They were probably hurrying out before the crowd slowed them down, hurrying so they could hurry to the next stopping place on their lists.

For several days I had been thinking, "Why has this

year gone by so fast?" Now I think I have the answer. We people are rushing through life so fast that time has to rush just to keep up.

Now, all too soon, 1987 is gone. Are we going to take the fast lane through 1988, too, or are we going to take time to savor the good things of life — many of them free?

At this time of year the news media spend a lot of time rerunning the events of the past 12 months. I'm not going to do that in these last Moments written in 1987. Just as we shouldn't rush through the new year, we shouldn't drag along all the worries and heartaches of the past year. Not if we want to go forward with courage and hope.

While shopping for a Christmas gift for a special friend, I leafed through a book of poems by Emily Dickinson. Before she died in 1886, she had written hundreds of poems. She called them her "letter to the world." She was considered a recluse and an eccentric, but she took time to appreciate the world and people with all their flaws and imperfections.

In one of her poems, there are two lines that express so beautifully what I have struggled in several paragraphs to say: "Look back on time with kindly eyes. He doubtless did his best."

The only way I could improve on that would be to add: "Doubtless she also did her best." After all, isn't that what all of us are trying to do?

Perhaps Emily's advice is a good way to start 1988. So, Happy New Year everyone.

CROSS THE GENDER GAP

August 1988

Too soon old — too late smart! I think that's a German expression (if it isn't I'm sure someone will correct me). Anyway, its meaning is clear in any language. The smarts we learn as we grow older are often late in making much of a difference in our lives.

This was a thought I pondered today as I tried to decide how to secure my backyard gate. The two-pronged clasp that fastens the gate is held by two large screws in the siding of my garage. The screws had worked loose and softened the wood around them so it was impossible to get them to hold. Starting new holes is too difficult for my inexperienced (and arthritic) fingers.

Why is it so difficult for women to do these repairs that seem to come naturally to men? As a little girl I used to watch my father sharpen tools on a grinding stone attached to a foundation with pedals. I can see him now, leisurely pedalling as he held the knives, hoes and whatever needed sharpening against the stone. Sparks would fly and there was a whining similar to that of a sawmill that operated just across our creek.

In later years I watched my brother repair ropes that pulled our water buckets from the well. He seemed to know how to do anything mechanical or electrical. He built our first radio from old sets others had thrown away. He put together his first automobile with a second-hand engine and body parts he rescued from the town dump.

Still later, I married a man who knew how to rewire lamps, repair furniture and make bookshelves. Being of the female gender, none of my early training involved such things as tools, bits and braces, splicing ropes. Oh, I learned at a very early age to cook (however, both of my sisters married bakers so they didn't bother teaching me how to bake) and sew. Why, at age 8 I could stitch a fine seam and make French knots. I learned to hold my fork with the prongs down and hold my knife properly, not to talk with my mouth full (something I now sometimes forget) and other manners.

I learned to iron, first with the sads and then the electric, to sweep and dust (chores I've hated all my life), to wash dishes (another tiresome occupation) and, when necessary, to make drapes and slip covers.

I learned all those things because my sisters thought those were the things girls would need to know when they became wives and mothers — so they told me.

No one bothered to tell me that one day I would be a widow who needed to know how to oil a fan or repair a light socket; who would need to know how to fill in the cracks of a new porch that had not been painted before winter set in — and now some of the boards are cracking.

If someone asked me for advice on raising a daughter and teaching her how to survive on her own, I would suggest she take a course in simple mechanics and manual training (I don't even know how to change a tire).

In these days of divorce and women outliving their husbands, chances are she'll need to know how to do a lot of things, unless she's wealthy enough to have them done. Even then she may have to do the follow-through. This past spring I hired a man to clean the gutters. My broom is still where he left it, on the roof.

If I had been smart, I would have learned those things from my father, my brother and my husband. I'm still learning by trial and error but it's harder. Oh, yes, about the gate fastener. I decided to try filling the holes with some wood glue and then putting the screws in. If it works maybe I'm not too soon old — yet.

WHO WAS FIRST?

October 1988

Last month we told you of the suggestion that we devote some Moments to the 19th Amendment to the U.S. Constitution. We asked you to share some thoughts (your own or those of ancestors) concerning anything related to women's suffrage and the amendment.

The response has been great. The first letter came from Martha Parriott with a story about her mother-in-law, Ethel Winnette Parriott, who carried the Kansas flag in the first women's suffrage march in Washington, D.C.

Ethel, just a girl at the time, was visiting in Washington with her mother. On the day of the march, the lady who was to carry the Kansas flag became ill. Ethel was delegated to march in her place.

Although she was not a Kansan at the time, she later moved from West Virginia to Wichita to be near her only son, R.B. and his family. Many Wichitans will remember this interesting lady who resided at Hillcrest Apartments and was active in P.E.O. and D.A.R. Thank you, Martha for sharing this story.

•••••

Maxine Adams, from the Wichita area, had a disillusioning experience at the polls when she was only 8 or 9. She accompanied her mother to a voting place in the first block on South Erie. Her mother was campaigning for a candidate. This was in the days when candidates and their workers were allowed to pass out campaign material at the polling stations. Her mother's candidate told Maxine, "If I would do this (pass out his material), he would buy me an ice cream cone."

She doesn't say whether he won the race or not, and she isn't positive about his name or the office he sought. She does remember, "For hours I passed out his cards, but when the time came for my reward he was too busy."

The candidate evidently was a Democrat for Maxine says, "That was the day I became Republican." I hope he lost the race, Maxine. Wouldn't it be wonderful if ALL politicians, Democrats and Republicans, kept their campaign promises? Then we would have no poverty, no wars, and best of all, no national debt.

•••••

And now a funny story about a young male chauvinist. Weston Cox of Newton recalls that several years ago the Freedom Train stopped in Tulsa, displaying original documents of U.S. history.

"When a schoolboy saw the women's suffrage amendment, he exclaimed, "Aw, those women haven't suffered." Weston declares the story to be true and I believe him. I seem to remember the train also stopped in Wichita and am I right in thinking that Lowell Thomas traveled with the exhibit? Anyway, thanks, Weston.

There just isn't space to include more letters, but I promise to try to include them all before we end this series. I've been reading some fascinating stories of the events leading up to the ratifying of the 19th Amendment. Who can tell me what state was the first to grant women the right to vote? I'll give you a little hint. It all started with a little tea party.

•••••

SOME MOMENTS TO CHERISH: The recent respite from the heat. The wilted four-o'clocks and hosta lilies were so grateful that they filled the air with such fragrance I wished I could bottle it. Botanica Gardens has been an oasis during the parched weather. Even the pudding-shaped flower beds at the Murdock House in Cowtown have braved the heat and dryness.

Until next month, remember: Age is an attitude, so keep yours optimistic.

KUDOS TO WYOMING

November 1988

What state was the first to grant women the vote? That was the question in last month's Moments. Two readers gave Kansas the honor but the kudos go to Wyoming and to a remarkable woman with an imposing name and intimidating physical attributes.

This fascinating bit of history has been related by a number of historians and Western writers. One of the most interesting accounts is in "Women of the West," a collection of well-researched and documented stories by Dorothy Gray.

"On Sept. 6, 1870 the women of Wyoming went to the polls and cast their ballots, the first time that women anywhere in the world exercised their right to vote as fully franchised citizens," writes Gray.

As I mentioned last month, this all started at a tea party. Considering that today many projects and decisions have their beginnings at cocktail parties, on golf greens and at bridge tables, a tea seems an appropriate setting for such a sober subject as women's suffrage.

After reading several versions of this important happening, I think it is safe to accept the statement that women's suffrage in Wyoming actually resulted from a tea party. The hostess is described as "six feet tall and weighing 180 pounds." Her name? Esther Hobart McQuigg Slack Morris.

Born in New York state in 1813 to a large family, she was orphaned at age 11, apprenticed to a dressmaker and married Artemus Slack, a railroad engineer, in 1842. She bore him one son. At his death (about 1845), he left Esther a tract of land in Illinois.

At a time when many states denied a woman the right to own property, Esther experienced great difficulties in assuming ownership of the land. The injustices of property laws made her aware of the need for women's rights.

Esther later married a merchant, John Morris. She bore Morris three sons and eventually moved with her family to the boom city of South Pass City, Wyoming. Within a year Esther launched the first successful drive for women's suffrage.

Her tea party was held in her home shortly before Wyoming's first territorial election in the fall of 1869. She invited two of the most promising politicians in the area, Democrat William H. Bright and Republican H.G. Nickerson, who were opponents for a seat in the newly formed territorial legislature. During the tea, she extracted from each man the promise that, should he be elected, he would introduce a bill for women's suffrage.

Bright, who won the election to head the territorial senate, kept his promise. On November 27, 1869, Bright introduced a bill that read, "Every woman of the age of

21, residing in the territory, may, at every election, cast her vote; and her right to elective franchise and to hold office under the election laws of the Territory shall be the same as other electors."

The bill (Council Bill No. 70), passed by the Democratic-dominated legislature and signed into law by Gov. John A. Campbell, fueled the fires that prompted other Western states to give women voting rights.

On February 14, 1870, Esther Morris' appointment as justice of the peace in South Pass City was considered "a true test of woman's ability to hold public office."

When Wyoming was admitted to statehood with its women's suffrage intact, Susan B. Anthony and other Eastern advocates of women's rights witnessed the event.

There are many theories as to why the pioneer states in the West were leaders in recognizing women's rights. Some of these will be included in the December Moments.

•••••

December 1988

Since this series on women's suffrage began, we have seen a hard-fought presidential campaign wind down. The candidates flew thousands of miles, criss-crossing the country to speak to hundreds of people. Millions more followed the campaign on office or home televisions.

During this daily exposure to television coverage, I found myself comparing the many forms of communication available to those open to the suffragettes.

It took days of train travel to reach cities that now can be reached by airplane in a matter of hours. Remote areas could be reached only by stagecoach, carriage, horseback or on foot.

It is no wonder that in 1867 three Eastern advocates for women's suffrage were defeated when trying to win voting privileges for the women of Kansas. They were Susan B. Anthony, Elizabeth Cady Stanton and Lucy Stone.

Anthony once found herself speaking to a handful of listeners in a drafty, half-finished church. Stanton's enthusiastic fight for her cause was dampened by nightly battles with the multitude of bedbugs that infested her third-rate accommodations.

And poor Lucy Stone. She traveled 40 miles a day in a springless carriage across rough roads to reach the little hamlets where she was lucky to catch the ears of half a dozen citizens.

Undaunted by their failure in Kansas, the women took their quest to South Dakota where, for three consecutive years, a drought had reduced the soil to a fine powder in which nothing would grow. Crops failed and cattle died from lack of food and water.

Their efforts were doomed to fail. Their timing was bad, Kansas was still licking its wounds from the border fights and the Civil War. South Dakota farmers were too dispirited to pay much heed to the rantings of "those Eastern females."

Their lack of planning and consideration of local conditions plus failure to form organizations on the grassroots level to pave the way for their campaign all contributed to setbacks that might have been avoided. And combining their fight for women's suffrage with their fight against "demon rum" weakened their cause.

Carrie Lane Chapman Catt, who assisted Anthony and her followers in the 1890 South Dakota campaign, was wise enough to see the futility of stumping in sparsely settled regions where there had been no planning.

Discouraged, she withdrew from the campaign until she was approached by the women of Colorado. They beseeched her to assist them in passing a referendum on women's suffrage. Assured of the backing of a strong organization and at the urging of her husband, George Catt, she rose to the challenge.

Carrie gained the admiration and respect of the male population by her display of courage in what became know as "Carrie's wild ride."

On her way to an important speaking engagement in the mountains of Colorado, her train was stopped by a wrecked train blocking the tracks. Unwilling to miss her appointment, she pinned her hat firmly to her head and, with a sack of sandwiches at her feet, boarded a hand car, which she steered through the night to fulfill her engagement.

Her courage and determination surely had a bearing on Colorado's victory in 1893. Three years later, her home state of Iowa gave women the right to vote.

After years of failure, the suffrage movement began to gain support. After Colorado and Iowa capitulated in favor of women's suffrage, Idaho followed suit, along with Utah in 1896, California in 1911, Arizona, Kansas and Oregon in 1912, Alaska in 1913, and Nevada and Montana in 1914.

Strange that Eastern women who fought so hard for the movement found their foothold in the Western states while their home states continued to resist.

•••••

January 1989

Last month we discussed the fact that, while Susan B. Anthony and other women of the East led the fight, the Midwestern and Western states (including Kansas) were the first to allow women the right to vote.

Why should this be so? After reading opinions of several writers who studied the subject, I think we have to give pioneer men a lot of credit for having the good sense to recognize that the women deserved this measure of equality.

After all, many of these women left comfortable homes, loved ones, their security, to go with their husbands to an unknown future. They bore their children in the wilderness, they shared the heat, cold and ofttimes hunger with the men. They learned to make soap, to dye clothes with colors from weeds, to sew, to patch, to fight locusts and when necessary, to plow fields and harvest crops.

Surely they deserved the right to vote.

LOST: ONE BUSTLE

March 1989

Has anyone see my bustle? I've lost my bustle ... or rather, I've lost Julia's (also Victoria's and Rea's) bustle. Actually I think the bustle was stolen while Julia stood on my front porch during the Christmas holidays. Before you begin to wonder if Marie's Moments is suffering some sort of breakdown, I had better make a few explanations. As some of you may know, in my capacity as ambassador for Old Cowtown Museum, I portray three early-day Wichita women: Julia Munger, Victoria Murdock and Rea Woodman.

In my portrayals, I wear costumes of the 1870s. The three ladies share petticoats and ONE bustle. The costumes take up a lot of space and to ease the situation I keep Julia's costume, plus the petticoats and bustle, on a dress form in my front bedroom. Topped with one of those forms upon which wigs are dressed, this dress form is quite lifelike, especially when complete with hat and shawl. Quite often, visitors get a start when encountering Julia in my bedroom.

One night before Christmas I was expecting some carollers from Old Cowtown Museum's Re-enactors, and I thought it would be a nice touch to have Julia on the front porch to welcome them. The carollers did come and two stayed for hot cider and cookies. It was well after midnight when I remembered to return Julia to the bedroom.

It was about a month later when I missed the bustle. I was scheduled for an early morning program for one of the church circles in Westlink. I was going to portray Rea Woodman and I planned to wear the bustle. I reached under the skirts and petticoats but all my hand encountered was the wooden frame on which the form sits. No bustle. I searched around the base of the frame, thinking the bustle might have slipped. But the bustle was GONE.

I was sure I had not removed it but I made a thorough search in the clothes closet, all around. No bustle. What to do? I needed that bustle to fill out the back of the dress and to lift the skirts off the floor. Besides, for an 1870s lady to go out bustle-less was unthinkable. I tried an ordinary pillow — too large. I tried a throw pillow — too small. Then I remembered my neck pillow that I sleep on. With shoestrings attached to the sides, the little pillow made a really neat bustle.

So now I don't really need the old bustle, but I hate to lose it. That bustle has been many places with Julia, Victoria and Rea. Whoever took it has taken what might have been the first bustle to make an appearance in

Wichita since the early days.

Maybe I should contact Bob Getz. He seems to have a knack of getting stolen property returned. There is no reward but I promise, if the bustle is returned, there will be no questions or punishment — not that I suspect any of you AA readers of such a dastardly deed.

WHERE THANKS ARE DUE

September 1989

When the Coleman Co. was sold, it occurred to me many people throughout the country have benefitted from this company. I am one of those people and for that reason I would like to share my memories of Coleman products and the Coleman family.

There are others far more qualified than I to write the history of the Coleman family. I offer my memories as a way of saying "thanks" to a company that has done so much for so many.

The memories cover a good part of my life — beginning long before I was aware of a state called Kansas or a place called Wichita.

They begin with coon hunting in the Ozark hills back of my home when I was a small child. Coon hunting was a favorite weekend sport of the menfolk, including my brother and brother-in-law. The hunters wore jackets with deep hems into which they stuffed gun shells, matches, tobacco and apples, leaving their hands free to carry guns and a lantern.

Mostly they were coal-oil lanterns until a salesman (they called them "drummers" in those days) sold Coy Hill a newfangled Coleman lantern. From then on, the

"Coleman" became a status symbol that burned brighter, even during the highest winds and, according to my brother-in-law "hisses so loud it scares off panthers and mosquitoes." Mosquitoes and panthers were plentiful in the Ozarks.

Some 20 years later (during the '30s) I really learned to appreciate Coleman products. While we were trouping in the sparsely settled Dakotas, a Coleman lantern lighted our house car (an early-day version of a mobile home), a Coleman camp stove furnished warmth for the frosty nights, and a Coleman iron kept our clothing presentable.

That iron was a fiery, spitting and sputtering monster that must have weighed 5 pounds (or so it seemed). There was no heat regulator for the different kinds of materials, so you had to work fast. But it certainly was superior to the old sadirons.

I doubt we ever gave much thought to the inventor of those items, which helped make primitive conditions a little less so. Once we had progressed to a more affluent lifestyle (indoor plumbing and electrical appliances) we forgot about them, although my husband once wished for a Coleman lantern when a storm caused an overnight electrical outage.

When we moved to Wichita in 1942, I took a job as a room clerk at the Broadview Hotel. We lived on Victor Place, and I had to board the bus at the corner of Hydraulic and Douglas — surely the windiest corner in the city. The wind could blast you in the back and blow dirt in your face at the same time.

One winter morning I stood with three other women waiting for the bus. The weather was miserable, the bus was late, and we were going to be late for work.

A big touring car pulled up to the curb and a horn honked. "Oh, it's Mr. Coleman," one of the women exclaimed. "Come on, ladies, hop in," a voice called. Not knowing if I was included, I stepped back while the others hurried into the back seat of the car. "You too, young lady," the voice called; and the front door opened for me. I needed no urging. I found myself seated by a handsome elderly gentleman with snow-white hair and one of the friendliest faces I had ever seen. Several rides later I learned this was W.C. Coleman, the inventor of all those products that had eased the earlier days of my life.

In the years to come I was to learn more about this remarkable man who "knew every one of his employees and their families by name." And I was to become acquainted with other Coleman family members.

When my husband was dormitory secretary at the YMCA, Clarence Coleman could always be counted on for a trophy for the chess club or a donation to the YM Boys Club.

Many times when I needed help with a story for The Wichita Eagle or The Wichita Beacon, I could count on Mrs. Sheldon (Gayley) Coleman's advice. She is well-named (I believe Gayley is her family name), because she has a great sense of humor and interest in life.

When there was a conference or a project, the Colemans could always be counted on for support. When the Wichita Press Women hosted the national convention, one of the highlights was a backyard party and barbecue at the Sheldon Coleman home.

But more than these memories of the Colemans and the social side of their lives, I know I am safe in saying the family has contributed greatly to the financial, educational and cultural growth of Wichita. The Coleman family has been generous in its support of philanthropic and humanitarian agencies. The Coleman Co. has provided income for thousands of people.

BOLT FROM THE BLUE

October 1989

The block on Riverside where I have lived for more than 30 years is usually quiet and restful. A block from the bus line, it is less traveled and has a small-town atmosphere, a place where the abundance from backyard gardens is something to share with those who have no gardens, where the illness of one neighbor is the concern of all.

So, when this tranquility is shattered, as it has been for the past few weeks, I find myself a bit on the nervous side ("stressed out" is the popular expression).

Heavy rains caused water to seep into my basement — not a large amount but enough to make me wonder if my basement walls are going to crumble.

Just before Labor Day, workers moved into the block and with those heavy shovels (backhoes?) and those things they use to break up concrete (air hammers?), the workers proceeded to dig holes in our parking and driveways to remove and replace water pipes.

When it came my turn, they failed to warn me that the water would be cut off for several hours. So here I was, with water in my basement but none to drink, to make coffee or to wash my teeth. Minor inconveniences.

As of now, the pipes have been replaced and the workers have moved on, leaving behind the piles of dirt and unfilled holes. I have been assured that they will replace the dirt but at present our block has the appearance of giant gopher holes.

There's more, folks, namely the Big Bang. Make that BANGS! There is a saying that lightning never strikes twice in the same place, but how about three times (almost) in the same place and in a matter of minutes.

This shattering event took place about 9 p.m. during a heavy rain. I was sitting in the front room trying to ignore the thunder and lightning (storms have always made me uneasy). Libby the cat was snoozing alongside me on the divan.

Suddenly there was a tremendous bang and a blinding light. Then another. And another. Sparks were shooting everywhere. My first thought was that lightning had struck my porch and my house was on fire.

I opened the front door. There was a sulphur-like odor. When I stepped out, I skidded on a wad of chewed-up wood pulp. There were chunks of wood and slimy pulp all over the porch, and I could see that one of the elm trees in my neighbor's parking had been hit. A neighbor warned me to stay indoors until the storm subsided.

Later I learned the extent of the damage. The tree nearest my own parking had been struck by a bolt that zigzagged to the tiptop. It then had struck the other side and jumped to an opposite tree before going underground. It followed the water line into my neighbor's basement where, according to her son, it lit up the whole basement before fizzing out. Two blackened patches of grass on the lawn mark the spot of entry.

I was frightened when the lightning struck but later, I was even more frightened to realize how close we were to having our homes destroyed and ourselves killed. I think we all need a good jolt now and then to remind us how vulnerable we are.

Oh, yes, at the first bang, Libby leaped into the air. Much later I found him cowering under the bed. Today the sun is shining, the noisy equipment has moved into the next block. More than ever I appreciate the peace and quiet of this block.

The pungent odor of herb vinegars and the mellow fragrance of apple mint jelly fill my kitchen, helping me forget the musty basement. A lovely late yellow rose in a blue bottle on my windowsill lifts my spirits on this muggy day. And a newly baked loaf of bread from Roslyn's kitchen reminds me of the many blessings I enjoy.

THEY COULD BE DEADLY

February 1990

These are not the kinds of Moments I like to share, but if you can profit by them, the sharing will be worthwhile. Do you have a bedside table where you keep a book to read when sleep won't come? A place for tissues for nighttime sniffles and perhaps a glass of water and your medicine?

Is there anything on the table that could threaten your life if taken accidentally? If you aren't positive, please check that table now and remove anything that could be remotely dangerous. Please! Everyday someone becomes ill, even dies, from accidentally ingesting a poison or dangerous drug. It could happen to you. It did happen to me.

One morning during the holidays I awoke with a sore throat. Recognizing the symptoms of flu, I mixed my favorite gargle (a teaspoon each of salt, soda and boric acid in a glass of warm water), called my friendly pharmacist for a refill of my cough medicine and made a pot of soup. I felt that having started treatment early, I would be well over the flu in time to enjoy holiday festivities with my friends.

I was having some sinus problems, so along with my cough syrup, I had a bottle of eucalyptus oil handy to sniff should I awaken during the night with a stuffy nose.

Things were going well until one morning (about 5:00) I awakened with a hard coughing spell. Without turning on the light I reached for my cough medicine, uncapped it and without bothering to measure, tilted the bottle and downed a teaspoon or more of oil of eucalyptus!

The next few hours are a blur. I remember the panic, the fiery burning sensation in my mouth and in my throat as the oil slipped down. In my panic, I wondered how serious is it? Am I going to die? Should I call 911?

But there was no time for thinking. There was the immediate necessity of getting to the bathroom, then the impossibility of getting out of the bathroom long enough to get to the telephone. It was late morning before I managed to call my friend Nancy, who came as fast as traffic would permit.

My doctor was not on duty and Nancy was advised to call the Poison Control Center for advice. The center records reported several cases: one woman died after ingesting a small amount; a child had lived after ingesting five teaspoons. Others had been very sick but had survived. By now eight hours had gone by, so it seemed the initial danger was over. But I was very sick.

It took three weeks before I could be "up and about." My taste buds are still numb and my mouth red and raw, but I'm experiencing hunger. Best of all, I'm beginning to take an interest in life again.

I've thought long and hard about sharing this incident with you. One doesn't like to admit such carelessness, especially at my age when such actions could be considered the onset of senility.

My doctor was pretty emphatic in telling me, "It could have killed you." But just in the past few days I have heard of two similar cases involving a friend (considerably level-headed) who took the wrong medicine with frightening results, and a young mother who had a glass of bleach and water next to a glass of plain water. She reached for the bleach water and got a big swallow before she realized her mistake.

All of this reminded me of something a doctor told me several years ago. A patient of his had died of what was considered a suicide. She had taken an overdose of sleeping pills. The doctor was sure that it was accidental. "I have warned her to keep them locked up. It is very easy for a person, not fully awake, to take them again, even twice, in the same night."

So, please, be careful about the kinds of things you keep on your bedside table or dresser. They could be deadly.

THIS IS THE BEST TIME

June 1990

Dear readers, we've shared a lot of Moments in this column ... good, bad, happy and sad moments. And now, as I approach a special year in my life, I have a lot of "remember whens" to share ... 80 years worth! Because, (as my husband used to say) "the good Lord willing and the creeks don't rise," come June 1, 1990, I will be celebrating the big "Eight-O."

I'm having trouble believing it — I don't feel 80. At least I don't feel the way I used to think I would feel at this age (should I live so long). In fact, when I was 35, I expected that by age 60 I would be a doddering old lady, shuffling along in my shawl and house slippers, my eyes and hearing gone, eating milk toast and cream soups (probably through a straw).

I certainly didn't think that 20 years past 60 I would still be driving a car, cooking my own meals, mowing my own lawn and sitting up past midnight to write this column because I was too busy to write it during the day.

But here I am and, the good Lord willing — you know the rest — hoping I can learn word processing to write the Great American Novel and welcome in another century.

Actually being 80 is no big deal anymore. Just look at all those 90-plus birthdays you see listed in Active Aging. I can't really prove I was born since the doctor didn't issue a certificate of the event. I'm not even sure there was a doctor.

In those days, babies were usually delivered in the home and often by a midwife. But an aunt, who lived nearby at the time, assures me I was born in the hottest June on record.

If you were around that early, you probably remember coal-oil lamps, wood-burning cook stoves, homemade lye soap, wearing Union Suits (long johns to the ski bums), putting your hair up in rag curls, outdoor toilets (privies).

Monday was wash day, Tuesday was ironing day,

Wednesday was mending day (what were Thursday and Friday?) and Saturday was baking day.

Do you remember sorghum molasses? Molasses cookies were my father's favorite. He would sit at the kitchen table with a pitcher of milk and as fast as the cookies came out of the oven he would dunk and eat, dunk and eat until my sister (who did the baking) would say, "For heaven's sake, Papa, leave some for the rest of us."

There wasn't a telephone or electricity in our house (and never running water) until I was about 10. And, of course, no refrigerator. Since we lived across Gar Creek (just a few blocks from downtown) we didn't get home delivery of ice. So my brother would haul it in his wagon, running fast to keep it from melting.

Remember the wonderful Fourth of July picnics with fried chicken, potato salad (no one worried about spoilage with those appetites), tomatoes, onions and cucumber sliced into vinegar water, pies, cakes, home-made ice cream and lemonade? We kids would break off branches of the elderberry bush to shoo away the flies.

All was not fun. There was World War I, the war to end all wars. We saved tin foil (I don't remember why), did without coffee, sugar and many things.

I remember the day my cousin Ben, who played the tuba in the hometown band, left on the troop train. Uncle John sat for hours on the front porch, polishing and polishing that horn.

My father died during the great flu epidemic, shortly before the signing of the Armistice. He knew all about war, having fought for the Confederacy and having been imprisoned. His last wish was for the war to end.

Remember the songs of that period? "It's a Long Way to Tipperary," "Over There," "Pack up Your Troubles in Your Old Kit Bag." I'll bet you remember dozens more.

We were such a patriotic people in those days. I remember how the old soldiers would march so proudly in the Armistice parades. Red Skelton's portrayal of the Old Soldier always brought tears to my eyes.

My older sister went away to be married during that war. I remember her "going away" suit. It was dark green with a fitted jacket and long tight skirt (they called them "hobbles"). She couldn't step high enough for the train steps so the conductor had to lift her aboard. I remember she wore gray spats — very stylish in those days.

Let's jump ahead to 1924. I'm now a teenager with spit curls, wearing those dresses with a dropped waistline and almost no skirt, showing rolled stockings just below the knee. It was the flapper era.

Remember those days: "oh you kid" … "you're the cat's meow" … "the bee's knees" … "my honey bun." We danced the Charleston, the Black Bottom and, if I remember correctly, the Turkey Trot.

By now we had electricity. My oldest sister had a light put on the front porch with a switch inside the house. When my other sister Rosa's boyfriend (we called them beaux) stayed too late, older sister would turn on the light, often catching the couple smooching (we called it spooning in those days).

Cars were scarce in those days. We walked or rode on the handlebars of our boyfriends' bikes. One girl in our crowd got to drive her stepfather's car — an open-air job with button-on side curtains in case of rain or snow.

Cars had running boards, bumpers and, oh yes, rumble seats. Remember!

And remember the silent movies — the scary serials "Perils of Pauline"; "The Iron Fist" (or was it Hand?). What a thrill when talking pictures came in (in color). And, yet, I recently saw the modern version of "Phantom of the Opera." It didn't hold a candle to the silent version. Remember the wonderful actors and actresses of the silver screen?

And what about the comic strips, funnies, we called them. And they were — The Katzenjammer Kids, The Gumps, Mutt and Jeff, Happy Hooligan — I'll bet you can name dozens more.

But it wasn't all sweetness and light. There was the Great Depression, another war to end all wars and still other wars. There were the horrible atrocities of the concentration camps. There were shortages (remember standing in line for a roll of toilet paper?).

Then there was the assassination of a president and of a president-hopeful. But then there was the "One Giant Step for Mankind." Nylons replaced the horrible rayon stockings.

We've seen both good and bad. And now, with all our progress, we have crime on the streets, drug abuse, pollution and endangered species.

Looking back, it seems that we were happier in the teens and twenties before all the big changes — the quick mixes, the charge plates, the computers — before the high-tech age.

Hopefully, with our memories, we can help young people to appreciate things that still make life worthwhile in a world that's spinning too fast. The beauty of a Kansas sunset. The enchantment of a baby's smile. The uplift of a church choir. The solace of prayer. And the hugs of good friends and loved ones.

If we older citizens can do that, we can say, "This is the best time of life."

SO MUCH TO DO

July 1990

The memories linger on! Three birthday balloons float over the TV, another attached to a flower-filled coffee mug dances at the dining room windows, stacks of birthday cards and gifts, two corsages alongside a bottle of wine in the refrigerator and a slice of birthday cake — 80th birthday memories to last a lifetime.

When I think of the planning, the work, the expense and the special caring that went into making the occasion so memorable, my eyes fill with tears and I feel very humble.

Should I live to be 100, nothing can top my 80th birthday. One of the things that made the event so special was having my youngest stepdaughter here to share the festivities with me. With no children of my own, I'm very lucky and grateful to have three stepdaughters, their children and grandchildren as my family ... my friends.

Several times I've been asked, "Had you known you would be around to age 80, would you have done anything differently?" and "What advice would you give to others facing old age?"

To the first question: I doubt I would have done anything very different. Looking back over the years, it seems to me that circumstances play a major part in shaping our lives — the nurturing (or lack of it) during one's early childhood and young adulthood, depression, wars, the environment — all those things that affect our physical and mental health, our illusions and attitudes.

I made a lot of mistakes (I still do). I didn't always use good judgment in coping. I made a lot of wrong choices that resulted in deep guilt feelings. But I like to think I learned enough from my mistakes not to repeat them too often. I did learn that guilt can be a crippling emotion, that one needs to ask forgiveness and then to forgive one's self.

For every up and down of life there are compensations. Without hardships, how can one appreciate the good things that come our way? Without illness, how does one understand the pain of others? Without grief, how does one learn compassion? I've been so lucky. I've had interesting, rewarding work, love and friendships that have enriched my life. Why change all that?

What advice would I give to others facing old age? If you have good health you don't need any advice from me. You have the energy and the time to explore new avenues of learning, to do so many things that less fortunate people can't do.

In any event, keep involved, if not physically then mentally. There are so many wonderful books to read or reread. If your eyes are not too good, investigate talking books or enroll in one of the radio programs for the vision-impaired. Senior Services offer wonderful programs and activities for older people. Older people have more going for them at this time than in any period in our history.

If your own family is tired of listening to your advice, there are plenty of young men and women who have no one to go to for advice. Ask your minister how you can use your years of experience to help others. I'm

sure he would be glad to have someone share his load.
There is so much you can do. Keep busy, but take time to
smell the flowers.

I guess the best way to face old age is head on — making the most of each day. Years ago, when I was complaining about having too much to do, a very wise young woman
said to me, "Marie, better to wear out than rust out."

End of sermon.

IT'S NOT SO EASY

September 1990

"Plan your work and work your plan. That's the way
to get things done, Marie." That was the sage advice
given to me by my brother years ago. My beloved brother Matt who went to work at an early age, took correspondence courses to fill in the gaps in his education,
built his own house (all except the air conditioner) on a
mountaintop in Oklahoma, all his life, never stopped
working and planning. Just a few moments before he died
from a heart attack (on the way home from church) he
was telling his wife of his plans for the next day.

When I think of all he accomplished in his lifetime,
I have to believe he must have taken his own advice. I've
tried to follow that advice, I really have. I make lists of
things to do … I plan ahead. But it never seems to work
for me. Today for instance. This is Friday, the day I get
my hair done (in fact I'm sitting under the dryer as I write
this). After all, my hairdresser can't be changing his
schedule just because I didn't get this column written earlier in the week as planned.

Forget all the reasons why, on this day (August 10)

I am trying to beat the deadline clock (August 10) for getting my copy to my long-suffering editor.

Most of the reasons were human ones — extracurricular activities that exhausted me physically and dulled me mentally. Five hours of sleep just doesn't do me anymore.

But some of the reasons have more to do with what folks in show biz refer to as "acts of God" or, more simply put, happenstance.

Today is also my day to water (lawn watering is still restricted in Wichita). I got up too late to do much morning watering, afternoon watering evaporates too quickly and I'll be gone for most of the evening (after all, I can't expect our bridge club hostess to find a substitute at this late date). Besides, I can't water too heavily today because tomorrow is the day the man comes to mow.

See what I mean? Early in January, I began to make plans for the months ahead:

• I began to get all the papers, bottles, cans, etc., sorted and sacked with plans to take them to the recycling center on the first Saturday of each month. But, it seems that on each first Saturday the weather was either too bad or something more important came up. On the first Saturday in July, feeling very smug, I got most of my stuff to the center. I guess my load was the last straw — the recycling volunteers called a halt. Now the stuff is piling up with no place to go.

• Another plan — to start spraying the weeds before they got a headstart. I bought the spray and the sprayer. A problem with the spray delayed the first effort, then the winds blew and the rains came. The weeds won.

• Time has blurred some of the other plans that went awry. One that surfaced recently was my failure to spray the evergreens according to plan. For the past few days I've had the unpleasant task of removing the bagworms and their clever tents that they build out of the greenery.

The rose bushes that survived the cold winter have not bloomed well because I forgot their feeding schedule. The flower beds are a weedy mess because I forgot to mulch.

But all is not lost. The herbs that I planted in a large pot are doing well (those in the back yard are being choked by the weeds. Only the mints are winning out).

Oh, yes, there are the four tomato plants that got planted according to plan ... well almost. I got them into a bed a week before the 100-plus heat. I nursed them through that period. They held on bravely, conserving their energy until the heat let up and a few rains refreshed them. One day I noticed they had started to grow and set on fruit. Yesterday I counted at least a dozen fruits (ranging from marble to golf ball size) and scads of flowers.

Maybe they were one of my better plans. Now summer is almost over. The four-o'clocks are blooming ... the cicadas have begun their nightly serenades ... the days are growing shorter. Might as well forget those early plans that didn't work.

Plans for the months ahead? Well, there are the gutters that didn't get properly cleaned last year (no use cleaning them until this year's leaves have fallen) ... there is the backdoor threshold that needs replacing (can't do that until it is cool enough to cut off the air conditioning and still warm enough to have the door open).

Planning is easy folks — it's working the plan that is so difficult. One good thing about all this (there is always SOMETHING to be thankful for) it gave me some moments to share (when the Moments I had planned fell through).

If you are still with me, my plans for October are to share with you some of my plans that have worked. Providing summer holds out long enough for the tomatoes to get big enough for piccalilli and the herbs hold off flowering long enough to make herb vinegar … and my memory holds on long enough to share some of the unplanned happenings that have made all the rest worthwhile.

WORKING THE PLAN

October 1990

Response to last month's Moments seems to indicate that a lot of folks have the same problems I have in "working my plan." A member of my Sunday School class said, if I would replace my name with hers the column would fit her "to a T," or words to that effect. Another said her mother read the column and advised her to "take heed or you'll wind up like Marie MacDonald." I'll bet that gave the daughter a jolt.

In rereading that column, I noticed I promised to tell you of some of the plans that DID work. As of now, I can think of only one — the vinegar works.

A few years ago, Frank and Mary Good took me to a meeting of the Herb Society, a fantastic group of men and women, young and old, all crazy about herbs. And soon I was addicted too, planting oregano, sage, savory, mints — prolific producers and soil grabbers.

To use up some of the surplus I tried my hand at herb vinegar. Two of my friends who were on diets liked the vinegar with oil for salad. I made up several bottles for our church bazaar, but not too many people were familiar with herb vinegars, so I ended up giving most of it to friends. They seemed to like it enough to save their bottles for refills. Then some of my bridge-playing friends tried it. Soon I had about 15 people saving up bottles for refills. That encouraged me to try other herbs and combinations.

Last summer I went overboard, planting basil (three kinds), thyme, tarragon, rosemary and five kinds of mint. Then, because of weather and unforseen problems, the herbs didn't do well. By the time I had gathered the vinegars (red, white and wine) and the large jars (vinegars need to ripen for several weeks before bottling), the herbs were past their prime. I tried to make too much too fast, ran out of jars (and space). My friends were too nice to complain, but I knew the flavors weren't all that great.

This year I was determined not to repeat that fiasco. Instead of planting in the garden spot (the oregano, sage and mint had taken over that space anyway), I planted basil, thyme and tarragon in a large clay pot. The tarragon didn't make it, but the other herbs thrived.

I got my vinegars and jars ready. Then as the herbs grew I made the vinegars in small batches. At the Farmer's Market I bought enough tarragon and rosemary to make a half gallon of each. These I will combine with other flavors. I also made some herb-garlic combinations for those who like garlic. I still have sage and mint vinegars to make and by now, I can bottle up what is ready and will have jars and space for sage and mint.

With suggestions from Kathleen Kelly, I hope to find rice vinegar in the half-gallon size for the mint vinegars. Regular vinegars are too overpowering.

This planning has worked so well that next year I plan to use pots for most of the herbs. That will save on watering and weeding and will be handier to my kitchen.

I guess the reason this plan has worked so well is I LOVE making herb vinegar! It is great for green salads and for marinating vegetables and meats. Sage vinegar goes well in bread dressings and (a bit) in dried beans and peas. Mint vinegar can be used in fruit dressings, and of course, on vegetable salads.

As a certain TV cook says, "Oooh, it's SO good."

BUT THE ENDING IS HAPPY

December 1990

One night in late October, a blond-haired girl, walking her dog along the west bank of the Arkansas River, was decapitated. The person, who used a chain saw for the dastardly deed, took the severed head away with him. The tape from a "Motley Crue" cassette was wrapped around the legs of her dalmatian dog. Several beer cans littered the area, indicating that there had been witnesses to the cruel scene.

How is that for a horror story opening? The decapitated woman was actually a wooden sculpture, so my description may be overly dramatic. Even so, this true story of senseless vandalism was shocking to many people.

Fortunately the story has a happy ending. For those of you who might not have heard of the vandalism, this is my account of the story. Wichita has had some destructive wind and electrical storms this year, destroying many of our beautiful trees. After one such storm I was saddened by the number of damaged trees in Riverside Park. They will have to be removed, I thought.

But, a few weeks later, when I drove through the park,

instead of broken tree trunks, sculptured wood figures of rugged men and women had sprung up in their place.

I marveled that someone had turned devastation into interesting works of art. I was even more impressed to learn that the talented sculptor (a young man from Peru) had actually carved those strong-featured figures with a chain saw.

My friend, Katie, who lives near the park, and I often talked about how much we enjoyed the art. When we learned that a new sculpture by this same artist was on the river bank we drove to see it. Crossing the Lewis Street bridge, we turned right and there she was, the Girl Walking Her Dog.

She had long yellow hair and wore a blue pants suit with a red blouse. In her hand was a chain attached to the spotted dog. They seemed to be patiently waiting for a lull in the traffic so they could cross the street. So lifelike, I just knew that a real live girl must have been the inspiration for this sculpture — someone the artist knew and loved. How nice of him to share her with passers-by.

Then, in a matter of minutes, she was beheaded. When the story came out in The Wichita Eagle with a picture of the artist, Gino Salerno, I could almost feel his pain. I was not surprised to read that his wife, Sharon, had been his model. How hurt and angry he must have been to see his work so shamefully treated.

And how remorseful the young vandal must have felt when he looked at that sad picture. (I say "he" because I can't imagine a girl wielding a heavy chain saw.) After the counselor of his high school returned the head to Mr. Salerno, the young man called the artist to repeat over and over, "I'm sorry."

As sad as it is to see vandalism, I believe we can take comfort in knowing this young person was contrite. We all (especially when young and under peer pressure) have surely done things we regretted. It must have taken a lot of courage for this young man to admit his guilt and to say, "I'm sorry." Hopefully, he has learned a valuable lesson.

Mr. Salerno seems to be a forgiving man. Just this morning I saw the Girl Walking Her Dog on the river with no evidence that her head had ever been anywhere except on her young shoulders. I'm glad the artist was willing to share her with us again.

PREPARING FOR THE NURSING HOME

September 1987

The Moments I want to share with you today are on the serious side but I hope they will help answer some questions for those of you who are facing putting a loved one in a care home.

Almost six years ago I had the responsibility of putting my sister in a nursing home. At first it was to be temporary until she recovered from a stroke. But additional strokes and problems made it a permanent stay until her recent death.

I was not prepared for the resentment and anger that my sister took out on me for doing what was necessary. I realize now that this is a normal reaction for a person who has been independent and her own boss to suddenly having someone else take over and make all the decisions. But as painful as it is, you must get a power of attorney in order to pay bills and, if the person becomes unable to write (as my sister did), to make decisions.

Be also prepared for daily reports of abuse and bad treatment. Don't be too quick to accept these as truths — but don't discredit them either. Just as there are good, bad and indifferent people, there are good, bad and indifferent care homes. I was so fortunate that in the two homes in which my sister spent her last years, she had, for the most part, good and loving care.

I did check out her complaints by going in at odd times (when few of the staff knew me), observing how she was being fed, standing in the hall and listening to the conversation while she was being dressed or given medicine. I walked down the halls behind a nurse or aide pushing a wheelchair or otherwise assisting a resident. Many times I would hear them using words of endearment and, in most cases, giving the same kind of care one would expect from a family member.

In the beginning I visited Rosa daily until a nurse pointed out I wasn't giving my sister a chance to adjust, to make friends, to rely on the nursing staff for her needs. When I spaced my visits, Rosa began to play bingo, attend movies and participate in crafts. One of my most treasured gifts from her is a ceramic high-top shoe she painted for me for Christmas. A recreational director and another staff member became her close friends, a friendship that followed her and was her (and my) comfort during her last days.

Being a proud and neat person, she looked forward to the days when someone (often a volunteer) gave her a manicure. She liked having her hair done. These little things mean so much to a person in a care home.

The idea of having her clothing marked was repugnant to her and to me. But this is a fact that must be accepted and considered when buying clothing. For a person who needs help in dressing, clothes that are loose and easy to get into are preferred.

There will be losses and there isn't a whole lot that can be done about it. All clothing is itemized when the person is admitted. Check with the laundry before you report a missing item. Don't always assume that a staff member has taken the item. Some residents, like children, wander from room to room taking something that catches their fancy. It is impossible for the staff to keep an eye on every resident every minute.

Some homes provide safekeeping for jewelry and money. When that is possible, it does help the resident's self-esteem to have a few dollars available to buy something or invite a friend to eat a meal with her. Having a meal now and then gives your loved one a feeling that she/he is treating you (even though you must pay for the meal). It also gives you a chance to judge the quality of the food.

•••••

October 1987

When admitting a relative (or even yourself) to a care home, be prepared to supply a full case history and medical records. Many homes also require that this person's doctor be willing to make house calls. This is a good and reasonable requirement. There are times when a resident's doctor needs to give a firsthand opinion in order that proper medication and treatment can be prescribed. Also the resident, particularly a new one, feels more secure when she knows her own doctor will be available when she needs him.

A requirement that startled me was the supplying of the name of a mortuary to be responsible for the removal of a body immediately following a resident's death. As cold as this seems, there is a necessity. There is always a certain amount of anxiety on the part of other residents when one of the care-home family dies, particularly for the resident sharing the room with the deceased.

Also, Kansas law requires the embalming, cremation and/or burial of the deceased within 24 hours. Most care homes require that room and board be paid in advance. Make sure you know what this payment includes, especially what nursing care is provided without extra cost. Take no chances. Learn as much as you can about requirements and policies.

More important, remember that policies CAN and often DO change. Had I remembered that, I might have saved myself some stress and my sister some painful adjustments.

The first home Rosa went into accepted Medicaid patients, and I was assured that if her money ran out while she was a resident there, she would be put on the program and receive the same care as a private-pay resident. Although Rosa's savings and Social Security had been adequate for her moderate lifestyle, I knew that a few years in a nursing home could quickly reduce her income. So I was relieved to know that she would be cared for under Medicaid.

By the end of three years she was fast approaching the $1,500 she would be allowed to keep. I had observed that the home did give the same good care to Medicaid residents and once again was grateful.

Then quite by accident I learned that sometime during that three years the home had gone OFF the Medicaid program. A check with the management verified the fact. I was angry that I had not been informed and I was frightened for my sister's well-being. After some frantic checking of what I needed to do, I got an appointment with a man at the Social and Rehabilitation Services (SRS).

He was most sympathetic and helpful. He had me fill out all the necessary papers so that Rosa could be put on Medicaid the day she was eligible. He gave me the names of care homes that would accept Medicaid persons and advised me to get on their lists, for there might be a long waiting period. Fortunately I was able to get Rosa into a nearby home in a fairly short time.

The move was painful for her. She had made some close friends at the first home and now, once again, she was moved into a strange world through no choosing of her own. It was stressful for me, too, having to deal with a new staff, nurses and policies. Without the kindness and understanding of the SRS office and the new nursing home folks I would have been devastated.

I am no longer angry that I had not been prepared for this emergency. There were too many kindnesses shown to my sister and me at the first home to hold ill feelings. I realize that with the daily duties and problems of nursing care, communications often break down with resulting oversights.

•••••

November 1987

We are told that money cannot give us happiness, yet the lack or shortage of money often causes extreme anxieties and despair.

This is particularly true of people with problems of old age and health.

Since I began this series on nursing homes, I've had face-to-face discussions, letters and phone calls concerning these problems. Over and over they ask, how long will my money last (in a care home)? What do I do when the money runs out?

One wonderful caring husband of my acquaintance is beginning to have these concerns. His wife has been in failing health for many years and in and out of care homes much of the time. At the time of his retirement he had invested what he thought would be an adequate sum to meet the needs of him and his wife for the remainder of their lives. Now with the rising costs of nursing care and her deteriorating health, he is beginning to have doubts.

How long does the money last? It varies with the home and with the needs of the resident. I can offer only the costs of my sister's care as an example. These costs are for the 40 months my sister was a paying resident, sharing a room in one of Wichita's nursing homes. I believe these costs were pretty much in line with other homes for the same period.

When Rosa went into the home almost five years ago, the basic cost (room, board and minimal nursing care) was less than $900 a month. By the end of the year, the cost had risen to more than $1,000 a month.

One bad fall resulted in a week in the hospital, another necessitated a trip to the emergency room to set a broken wrist. Extra nursing care and bed meals added extra charges to her bill. Aside from that, the monthly charges continued to be well over the thousand-dollar mark. At the end of the 40-month period, her care home costs were more than $43,000.

Even with Medicare, Blue Cross and Blue Shield, she paid approximately $1,000 for hospital care. What really shocked me when I totalled these charges were her medical bills — more than $3,000. So for her 40-month stay, allowing nothing for clothes and toiletries, her charges came to more than $47,000. Is it any wonder people worry about money?

What happens when the money is gone? In Rosa's case, it was Medicaid. I may be wrong but I've always felt that my sister's Social Security and small pension (a total of $350 to $400) made it easier to get her on Medicaid and into another good care facility in a short time.

A reader from Burrton points out that Medicaid has been cut drastically, placing additional hardships on hospitals and nursing homes. This in turn affects the Medicaid participant. She feels strongly that this should not affect the way in which care home residents are treated, stating, "It doesn't cost any more to give a patient decent treatment."

But it does affect the number of qualified nurses and nurse aides that some nursing homes can afford to hire. The pay for these workers is generally lower than is paid by hospitals, with the result that many nursing homes are understaffed or must make do with less-qualified workers. And this affects paying patients and Medicaid patients alike.

One reader wrote some very scary stories of things that happened to her husband as a result of shortage of help. In the last stages of Lou Gehrig's disease (unable to walk, talk or care for himself), her husband had a broken hip, broken knee and multiple bruises resulting from being dropped repeatedly while being given showers by a nurse aide. She quoted the aide, "I knew I shouldn't be bathing him alone but we've been short of help for the past week and I've had to do it by myself. I've dropped him every day. Maybe if you complain we'll get some help."

Of course she moved her husband to another home. He died at age 69 from what she considers "several years of living in hell." She continues to collect information on insurance company policies relating to nursing homes.

•••••

December 1987

I recently spent time with staff members at three nursing homes regarding policies and care. I was permitted to study materials put out by the state agency that sets up and governs care-home policies and standards.

The qualifications and training for licensing of nursing homes, their staffs and facilities are stringent and the standards must be maintained. Reports of violations are investigated and if proven true, can result in the care home losing its license and/or other considerations.

A resident can complain of personal neglect or some general neglect in the home. I was told that such a resident (or a person responsible for that resident) should first complain to the in-charge nurse on duty at the nurses' station. If the condition continues, complain to the head nurse and/or administrator. Someone noticing serious neglect should complain directly to the Kansas Care Home Association in Topeka.

On admittance, a new resident in a nursing home should be made aware of that home's grievance policy (Residents' Rights). Anything the resident does not understand should be fully explained. If any of these rights are violated, the resident has a right to complain and continue complaining until the situation is corrected.

IF I HAD IT TO DO OVER AGAIN: During the five years my sister was in a nursing home I visited her frequently, but usually for short periods of time. Rosa often spent most of that time voicing her complaints — of the home, her health, me, things in general. Perhaps, knowing I would be there for such a short time, she felt she had to get her complaints aired before I rushed away.

• If I had it to do over, I would concentrate more on the quality of my visit, staying for longer periods of time. Rosa loved to "visit" so I would make my stops "visits" rather than duty calls. I would take along some needlework and have her work at something too. I would take letters and pictures to share. The social services director made a wonderful suggestion: "Take a tape recorder." Rosa would have loved hearing messages from others, conversations, music and short programs. And she would have loved sending messages to her friends. When she could no longer write, I would take dictation for her letters.

• I would save jokes to share with her to make her laugh, and even share some sadness. By sharing emotions she would have felt a bigger part of my life.

• I would avoid visiting her when I was in a bad mood. She always sensed such moods and reacted accordingly.

• Instead of giving her advice, I would ask for hers, letting her know that her opinions were important.

•••••

Nursing homes are always in need of volunteers, and residents of those homes are always looking for someone to talk with.

A FLASHBACK

July 1991

Ofttimes when I am reading (my favorite pastime), a word will jump off the page to trigger a series of mental flashbacks — like turning the pages of a memory book.

Such was the case while reading a charming story of a Jewish couple, Rebecca and David, who took on a whole load of problems when they took a little black girl into their hearts and home. It was during the Depression and they were hard pressed for money. Rebecca had found a little house they could afford, but David pointed out, "We don't have money to make the move."

Rebecca said she would pay for it out of her "knippel," explaining to her astonished husband that her mother had taught her that all Jewish brides should build a knippel.

By saving a little from the grocery money ... walking instead of riding the bus ... little by little there would be money for a rainy day. David had not known about the knippel because, Rebecca quoted her mother, "Don't tell your husband."

I checked my Webster for an American definition for the word, but didn't find it — didn't need it. Knippel in any language means those pennies and nickels (sometimes a dime or quarter) hidden away by countless enterprising women under such names as nest egg, butter and egg money, or perhaps Mom's cache can, hidden in the far corner on the top shelf of the kitchen cupboard.

In my research of early Kansas women I've often encountered stories of how pioneer women built up their little nest eggs by "holding out" a small portion of money from the sale of (what else?) butter and eggs. They called this little deceit "my little secret."

The first knippeler to enter my memory bank was my Aunt Johnny (her father, who wanted sons, gave masculine names to his four daughters). She was a wonderful little woman whose only claim to fame was being a good wife, working like a slave and, as far as I know, never doing an unkind thing in her life.

In a way, Aunt Johnny was one of those pioneer women who lived all her married life in a tiny three-room log cabin on a farm three miles from town. She still made her own soap and boiled her husband's overalls in a big black kettle over an open fire.

Uncle Jim was a funny, lovable little man with short arms and legs. Blue eyes twinkled in the folds of his whiskery cheeks. He managed to raise enough cotton and corn for the necessities, but his heart wasn't in it.

He had been a prospector in his youth and had never gotten the gold fever out of his system. When Aunt Johnny saw him leaving with his pick and tow sack, she knew he was "off to prospect" in the Ozark hills. Most folks considered the old man "off" period.

Aunt Johnny seldom left the farm. She raised a small garden, including a patch of tobacco. I think she smoked a pipe, but I never saw her do it. If she did, it was probably her only vice. I don't think she ever saw a movie. She never complained about her life, but, I'm told, that in later years someone bought her a battery radio and that she would sit for hours enchanted by the music and dramas.

And she had her knippel. She seldom accompanied her husband on his wagon trips to town to buy supplies.

But, about once a month she trudged to town to sell sweet butter and clean, fresh eggs.

When the storekeeper paid her, she would carefully put the money into an old coin purse — all but one nickel. On her way home she would stop at my brother-in-law's bakery and buy a nickel's worth of cookies (he usually put in a few extras). Then Aunt Johnny would walk slowly home, savoring every morsel of her store-bought cookies.

She had many nieces and nephews, but I was lucky enough to be her favorite. Perhaps it was because I was lonely too ... without my mother. Maybe it was because I visited her a lot ... besides, I loved her.

Twice a year, on my birthday and at Christmas, Aunt Johnny would give me a little gift — a box of crayons, a storybook, once a lovely little doll. I never knew how she shopped for those gifts, but I did know they were paid for with money in that little coin purse — it was our secret.

My oldest sister, Emma, had a nest egg too ... only she called it her "bootee bag." Sister was a talented woman. She could draw, she could sing and she could make beautiful hats and clothes. Early in her marriage she fell in love with a coat in a Dallas shop window. As she hadn't had a new coat since her marriage, she had her heart set on that coat. My brother-in-law pointed out that they had just made a payment on the bakery and "honey-bun, we just can't afford a new coat this year." He didn't know my sister very well.

She had crocheted a pair of darling booties for a friend's new baby and that friend had shown them to another friend, who asked Sister to make a pair for her baby.

She agreed if the friend would pay her the money ($2.00) in advance. As you have probably guessed, the money was a down payment on a layaway for the coat. She was warned that if she didn't pay the balance by the end of the month, the coat would go back in the window.

For almost four weeks my sister crocheted bootees at night while her husband was at the bakery setting sponge for the next day's bread. Through her friends she found a ready market for the "cute bootees with pom poms." As the money came in (she was now charging $2.50) it went into a crocheted "bootie bag."

Her husband never knew her secret until the day she walked into the shop in her new coat. He was proud of her resourcefulness and suggested she make "bootees" a full-time job. But Sister was tired to death of making bootees, besides, she said, "I've run out of customers."

You don't hear much about nest eggs these days. Women's role has changed, often they are the bookkeepers of the family and consider it their right to have credit cards and a bank account. Even so, many women (and men, too) use their talents to earn a little extra money ... their pin money or mad money they sometimes call it.

INVENTORY TIME

January 1992

1992 — another new year! Time to take inventory. I'm not talking about counting the canned goods, the light bulbs, not even the pennies in the cash drawer. No, this is an inventory of those items stowed in your brain bank. Those components that make you uniquely YOU. Are there some shortages that need to be filled or some excesses that need eliminating? Are there some leftover attitudes formed by prejudice and poor understanding that need to be re-evaluated, perhaps recycled, or put through another rinse cycle?

Are there some phobias that are robbing you of enjoyment of life because you are unable to enter a crowded room, ride in a plane or pet an animal?

How about the grudges that you've been carrying from one year to the next — rubbing against your better impulses — warping your sense of humor, your capacity for love and forgiveness?

And along with those grudges, are you hampered by guilt that colors you blue? Maybe the grudges and guilt belong in the garbage disposal.

Are there old notions that need changing — old opinions that need reversing — old mannerisms that need to be replaced?

In other words, are the negatives in your life robbing you of the capacity to enjoy the things that make life worth living? Negatives, those forces that try to dominate your life, that put blinders on your eyes so that you only go in their narrow directions. Negatives are those hangers-on that drag you down and make you wonder why you are sometimes so soul weary.

How do I know? Oh my, I know firsthand about negatives — carryovers from misunderstanding, lack of mature reasoning, nurtured fears of insecurity.

Maybe you are one of those fortunate people who hasn't had to live with negatives — lucky you. But most folks I know have at least one or two negative bugaboos.

Wouldn't it be wonderful to clear all the negative clutter from our lives, to go into the new year feeling light and free! We can, of course, if we will dust the cobwebs from our gray matter and try to understand what is involved.

Take those attitudes about certain social problems — about what we feel is the right way to do certain things, how certain people should act in certain situations, how we dislike certain people. Do we really stop to analyze why we don't like certain people, certain actions on their part? Would it help if we examine our own shortcomings, would we be more tolerant of others?

Phobias are difficult to banish, but if we can understand what causes them, maybe we can deal with them and control them. I traced my own claustrophobia back to my childhood when, at about age 9, I was punished by being shut in a dark closet, where, hours later, an aunt heard my hysterical screams and unlocked the door. My fear of escalators probably is the result of being on a very old wooden escalator that suddenly stopped and pitched me off. I still have claustrophobia and I still dislike escalators, but I rarely let them dominate me.

Grudges and guilt are probably the most destructive of all negative forces. I saw grudges almost destroy a family. The grudge between two sisters alienated them from another sister and brother who didn't want to take sides. I have had a few grudges of my own until I saw they were hurting me more than the person on the receiving end.

Guilt can actually make you ill, and, I think, is the most difficult negative to avoid. None of us is perfect — most of us make bad decisions, hurt those we love, abuse friendships and say cruel things we regret. The experts say, and I believe them, the best way to rid yourself of guilt is first to forgive yourself for any wrongs you feel you have done, particularly to others, resolving, of course, to compensate for wrongdoings with some right doings.

Of course no one can do these things for us. We first

need to want to change our attitudes and other negative feelings and then go about trying to eliminate them.

I recently read about a woman who spent many years fettered by fears, prejudices and guilt. She finally joined a support group and was made to realize she needed to replace the negatives in her life with positives.

The things she did were so simple that anyone could do them, perhaps with some variations:

• Doing something she had never done before. She took off her shoes and stockings, hitched up her skirts and went wading with a bunch of kids — something she had wanted to do for years but was afraid it would be unladylike.

• Going someplace she had never been before — a jazz festival — music she had loved as a child but had avoided because some people considered it too uninhibited.

• Calling someone she had never called before — a talk show on a subject she knew nothing about but had always wanted to know. She found it fascinating and exciting.

• Making a new friend — a neighbor down the block, unhappy like herself — they had avoided each other because each thought the other unfriendly.

"As I began to make these positive moves, I realized how, for years, I had closed myself in my little narrow world. By changing I opened myself to the world and found it wonderful."

These are thoughts I want to share as we go into 1992. We can't ignore the ugly things that go on around us, blind ourselves to financial worries, terrible diseases, frightening storms and the needs of people around us. But, in each of us are strengths to deal with problems if we can hold on to our faith and the positives.

As a friend of mine said, "No matter how bad things get, there is always help if we remember to pray." What better way to start a new tomorrow.

CATCHING UP TIME

February 1992

January 1, 1992, was my kind of New Year's Day. Black-eyed peas, corn bread, cabbage and other traditional food along with good conversation with some special friends. What better way to start a new year.

But now it's catching up time. Skirts — the long and short of it — that's the topic for these Moments. And you can blame it all on the First Ladies. Remember in a recent column I asked your opinion on older women wearing miniskirts, saying, "I really need to know." For a while my question was answered with a question, "WHY do you really need to know?"

I hate being put on the spot like that, especially when if the truth be told, I had exaggerated a bit. What I really wanted to know (is) do you agree that older women shouldn't wear the really short skirts or am I being an old fuddy-duddy?

Though I'm a bit (a wee bit) on the far side of "older," I still like to be moderately up-to-date, fashion-wise. In the roaring '20s (yeah that far back), I wore my skirts above my knees and my stockings rolled below, a la Flapper Fanny style, along with the other teenagers who were doing the Charleston. Then, in the '60s when skirts went hiking up again, I went along with the inch (or was it two) above the knee (my legs were still pretty good). But, when they started higher I opted for pants suits.

This time around, thus far, I've gone the middle road — some a bit longer, some a bit shorter, but still well below the knee (what the younger generation probably considers "considerably dowdy").

But the skirts have gotten shorter and shorter until high water swimsuits and short shorts are very modest. But most of the women in the 60-plus age bracket were still holding the line, I thought.

Then came a day in November when I was asked to serve as a greeter for a function at Old Cowtown Museum where our own First Lady was scheduled to make an appearance. It was cold out there (20-ish with a brisk breeze). I was wearing a three-piece wool costume plus petticoats, bustle and thermal underwear, and of course, a head covering, gloves and cape.

I stood outside for almost two hours (with a few minutes break in the heated building). My nose, ears and toes were numb. It was almost time for me to leave and it appeared the governor wasn't going to show. I was ready to leave and then, coming toward me on the boardwalk were two men and a female (it was getting too dark to see features). I guessed her to be a young matron in view of the length of her skirt, barely peeping below a three-quarter length coat. I wasn't prepared with a proper greeting when the lady turned out to be our First Lady. I have to admit her legs looked pretty good.

I came home a bit sorry that our very first lady governor had chosen to wear such a short skirt, particularly on such a cold day.

WHAT WAS SO GOOD?

March 1992

So, what was so good about the good old days? That question was overheard (a nice word for eavesdropping) at a gathering of folks at one of those open-to-the-public free programs.

The discussion was between two middle-aged matrons about their complaining parents. "Mom's always complaining about things not being the way they were in the good old days ... the good old days for heaven's sake ... the Depression, the dust storms, the war rationing. She's always reminding me of how much better we have it than when she was raising a family."

"I know. I'm so sick of hearing what it was like not having a car ...

"Yeah, I get so tired of having her scold me about wasting food ... how tough it was back then. And, yet, she never goes shopping without grumbling about how different things were in the good old days ... makes you wonder."

The conversation ended with the appearance of the speaker. But that question, "What was so good about the good old days?" intrigued me and I tucked it into my memory bank for future contemplation.

I was reminded of it a few days ago when I stopped at Towne East to buy some hose. I wanted some dark blue hose to wear with a midnight blue skirt. In the department store there must have been 30 or more racks of hosiery, almost as many brand names and a variety of prices. There were almost as many shades of navy blue as there were brands and those in the packages never look the same as the samples that are supposed to show you the color. There was no salesclerk and when I finally did get the attention of one nearby, she let me know it wasn't her department but, if I made my selection, she would ring up the sale. As she waited impatiently for me to write my check, I found myself wishing "for the good old days."

What was so good about the good old days? Certainly not the dust storms, the Depression, the wars. No, it was the little attentions that used to make shopping such a pleasure. Whether you live in Wichita or one of the surrounding communities, I know you will relate to some of the following:

Remember when ...

You stopped at the wonderful old Innes Store! There was lunch at the Tea Room. What a delight to sit at a table spread with snowy linen, polished silver and sparkling crystal. You might have a fruit plate (fresh fruit topped with pomegranate seeds and honey dressing) with finger sandwiches. Or, my favorite, cheese souffle. There was usually a style show. And don't forget the finger bowls.

Lunch over, you stop at the hosiery counter where a trained saleslady tells you the best shades to wear this season. She takes a demonstration stocking, gently runs her hand inside so you can see what the shade will look like on your legs.

If you are a regular customer, she knows your size, your height and weight. Then chooses the correct size for you. None of that ABC stuff that never seems to fit the same way twice.

If it's gloves you need, you will probably walk a block to Buck's where you know the bag and glove buyer. She probably knows your size and price range, so she brings out several pairs from a dust-free case. When you've made your choice, she props your elbow into a velvet-covered pad and fits the glove onto your hand, carefully stroking each leather finger onto yours, making sure the glove fits snugly, but comfortably, on your hand. The purchased gloves go into a nice box between layers of tissue paper.

On the way out you remember you need face powder. At the cosmetic booth, there is a saleslady trained to blend several shades of powder to suit your particular complexion. And because you are a good customer, you get a tiny flacon of new perfume and several samples of creams that will be nice for that weekend trip you just mentioned you would be taking.

Remember when you needed a new bra or foundation garment, you would go to a department store where a trained saleslady took your measurements (in a dressing room of course), then brought in several garments for you to select from. She helped you into the garment, making sure it supported you in the right places and was comfortable. Then she helped you dress and sent you on your way, a satisfied customer.

Compare that with today's department store lingerie section where dozens of bras and girdles hang on racks to be pawed through and mixed by other frustrated customers. You make your own selection, find your own dressing room and fit your own body into the sometimes soiled garments.

Thank goodness Wichita still has a few specialty shops and dress shops where I do most of my shopping. I'm overwhelmed by racks and racks of clothing and where getting a salesperson's attention is stressful.

Perhaps the younger generations, never having had these little personal services that you and I knew in the good old days, don't miss them. Just as today's younger folks don't miss cakes baked from scratch.

But those of us who do remember those personal attentions miss them, just as we miss the home deliveries of milk and groceries ... and doctors who made house calls.

Personal attention, that's what was so good about the "good ole days."

A MEMORABLE THANKSGIVING

December 1992

It's funny how one memory triggers another ... and yet another. When my husband worked at the Y, we had been in Wichita for about five years, long enough to decide this just might be our home "for a while."

Now, as I write this, I realize that in just a few days I will be spending another Thanksgiving in Wichita ... my 50th. The weatherman is predicting snow, and I'm recalling our first winter here. It was 1942 and we were at war.

We were living in a two-room apartment in the LeRoy Hotel, just two blocks from the Broadview Hotel (I think it was on Water Street). I was working at the Broadview as a room clerk and my husband was a floor walker at Innes.

I don't recall where we ate Thanksgiving dinner that year, probably with some of the good friends who had helped us find jobs. What I do recall is an incident that happened around Thanksgiving season that was both amusing and sad.

There just may be some of you readers who worked at the Broadview in 1942 ... you might have been a bell-hop, a waitress in the coffee shop. If so, you might have heard some version of this story or you might have known the Chesley McCormicks. He was the manager, and he and his lovely wife (everyone loved her) and their young daughter lived in an apartment on one of the upper floors. This story is not meant to hurt or offend anyone. But if you did happen to be a part of this 1942 scenario, I think you will get a chuckle from this story.

I was working a split shift that included Saturday and Sunday, 7 a.m. to 3 p.m. When I checked out Saturday afternoon, the hotel was booked solid for a convention. Servicemen on a weekend pass from Fort Riley were begging to be put on stand-by for possible late check-outs.

The weather had turned miserable. It snowed during the night, and the biting cold wind made my two-block trek to the hotel difficult. The wind pushed me through the hotel door with such force that I almost fell over a heap that turned out to be the bodies of two servicemen asleep on the lobby floor.

In amazement I looked around the big room — everywhere, sleeping servicemen. On the divans, the chairs and mostly, on the floor, their coats and gear tucked around them. Some were softly snoring.

I recall one young man had a smile on his face as if enjoying a good dream, his face so young, so vulnerable. I made my way to the front desk where the night clerk was putting on wraps, eager to get home to a warm bed. I had seen her husband waiting outside in his car, the engine running.

"They started coming in around midnight," she explained. "They couldn't find a room anywhere and it was freezing outside. What was I supposed to do, turn servicemen out in the cold?"

"But what about Mr. McCormick, what did he say?" By now she was on her way to the front door. "Don't know. Didn't ask him," she turned and grinned at me. "Good luck with Mr. M."

Good luck, she said. I had been working at the hotel for about five months. Long enough to know Mr. M's temper and to know that it didn't exclude women. I was close to panic.

It was now 7:30. The coffee shop would be opening soon and the manager was usually down to check on everything before 8 o'clock. The night bell captain had gone off duty. The PBX operator was busy with wake-up calls. People would be coming down soon.

Jim, the night elevator operator, usually stretched out on a settee in the mezzanine between calls. He seemed my only hope. I dashed up the short flight of stairs and shook him awake. When he saw the situation he whispered, "Holy Ned, the boss'll split a gasket. C'mon." He pushed me into the waiting elevator and was halfway out the door when it opened again.

The next few moments were a blur, shaking shoulders, helping arms into coats, shoving men toward the men's room and into the now open coffee shop.

By now there was an ominous buzzing of the elevator. Then it stopped, and a moment later the PBX operator yelled, "Mr. McCormick has been buzzing for the elevator, he's on his way downstairs and he's mad as hell."

"Uh oh," Jim said, as he pushed the last serviceman to the coffee shop door. "Marie, get behind that desk and don't let on about a thing."

"What are you going to tell him?"

"I don't know, but I'll think of something," and he made a dash to the rest room.

I had just gotten back of the desk when I heard Mr.

M clattering down the steps. He wasn't a tall man, but he had attended West Point and "walked" tall. Except now, he wasn't walking. He skidded up to the desk as if on a skateboard. His face was red, and he was puffing like a steam engine.

"What the hell's going on here … what's wrong with the elevator? Where the hell's Jim?"

Jim came hurrying from the men's room. "Sorry Mr. McCormick," he said in his best placating voice. "I've been in and out of the john all night. Something must have disagreed with me. Sorry sir."

As if on cue, the front door opened and the day operator arrived in a flurry of snow. Mr. McCormick looked at the clock behind the desk and bellowed, "You're five minutes late." The elevator buzzed. "Get in there and get that elevator moving."

"Yes sir," the new arrival said. Still in scarf, gloves and overcoat he hurried into the elevator and shut the door. Having vented his spleen to his satisfaction, Mr. McCormick calmly turned to me. "Well, Marie, folks are sleeping late this morning. Looks like you're going to have a nice quiet Sunday."

With that he sauntered to the coffee shop and didn't see the several servicemen who sneaked out of the men's room and out the front door.

When I think of that incident, I smile and I also have a little prayer that all those young men made it back from the war.

FAREWELL PERFORMANCE

April 1992

My husband had a habit of teasing me by quoting Shakespeare when there was a serious decision facing me. The opening lines of Hamlet's famous soliloquy, "To be or not to be … that is the question," was often quoted during my many "can't make up my minds."

Well, as you read this Moments my decision, made two years ago, "not to be" has reached its conclusion. My more than 15 years as official Ambassador of Old Cowtown Museum will have ended March 30 with a farewell performance of Julia Munger at a reception held by the Cowtown Social Club.

Since Julia Munger was my first in-person characterization, it seems fitting that she should be my last. Julia and I have relived a lot of history during the past fifteen-and-a-half years.

It will be a bittersweet day for me, ending what has been a wonderful, rewarding experience portraying four women who had a significant role in the early history of Wichita: Julia Munger, a stalwart pioneer whose husband built the Munger house; Victoria Murdock, the gutsy wife of the founder of The Wichita Eagle; Rea Woodman, whose book "Wichitana" tells of the lifestyles of Wichita people during the 1870s; and Harriet Fisher, whose role as first president of the Wichita Women's Relief Society gave comfort to so many during a time of pestilence and depression.

It was my decision to terminate my Ambassador role, although I am sure there were those who felt it was high time. After all, I am now two years older than Julia Munger, who was 80 when she was laid to rest at

Highland Park Cemetery. The other ladies were in their 70s at the time of their demise. Like Hamlet, my choice was a difficult one, but I knew it was time. Aside from age and some health factors, drive-by shootings have made driving unsafe, particularly at night for a woman inhibited by a bustle and long skirted costume.

I will continue to be involved at Cowtown. I've become too attached to the little village to turn my back completely. I will be a volunteer. I may even do an occasional Julia or Victoria. But mainly, I hope to contribute to the research department.

And that brings me to the real reason for relating these Moments to you. The months of research I found necessary to portray women of the 1870s have made me realize how important it is to keep family records. Without the journals of such pioneers at James R. Mead, much of Wichita's early history would be lost to history professors and historical writers. Wichita is fortunate to have a city historian, Bill Ellington. But without someone to set down the historical facts in the first place, historians would be hard pressed to function.

In other Moments, I have encouraged you to keep journals of your own family. Now I'm going to make a suggestion I hope you will consider.

It may be a bit early to be talking about Christmas, but not too soon to start a Christmas gift for your family — your family history.

My friend Laura used to tell me wonderful stories about her life on the farm, her job in Hutchinson and about her parents and siblings. She often talked about writing the stories down for her grandchildren ... some day.

But, being a person with many interests, Laura kept

putting it off. Then one day she was wondering what in the world to give family members for Christmas. "I'm clear out of ideas," she said.

I reminded her of her plans to write about her family. "Put those stories in a book. They would make a wonderful gift," I said.

After spending a few days wondering if the family would find the stories as interesting as she did, Laura got busy, and with the help of a friend with a word processor, she got the history written and had copies made for her two daughters and their children. The results? They loved it!

Another friend recently told me that she had done the same thing for her children and they loved it. So why don't YOU? Not only will you be doing something for your family members, you will be contributing to the documenting of local history. So many of our history books are filled with dates, statistics and facts.

Valuable, true, but often dull, dull, dull. They lack the human touch that makes history come alive and exciting. Each generation's history is valuable to future generations. And each individual family history is unique, something badly needed in this computer-mad world.

Don't tell me you don't have anything interesting to write about. Your response to last month's Moments in which I lamented the personal attention so lacking in today's shops indicated the valuable memories you have to share with your grandchildren.

So put them down, along with pictures, clippings, invitations, programs, mementos — things important to your family today. Just think someday in the far off future, a grandchild or maybe a grand niece or nephew might say to his or her grandchild, "The reason this cake is so good, it is made from scratch, from Grandmother's journal." Or, "Let's try Aunt Mabel's idea for feeding the roses. Hers were always so beautiful." Or, "What was it Grandfather used to do to keep his tools from rusting?"

Or even a future history professor might find a bit of history in your journal that would be important to his class. As the old saying goes, "How can you know where you are going if you don't know where you've been?"

Above, Marie portrays Victoria Murdock at a church banquet in 1983.

Marie, left, wrote a column for Active Aging from 1981 to 1992.

Marie portrays Victoria Murdock, right, at the Sedgwick County Historical Museum in 1986.

Marie as Julia Munger at Old Cowtown Museum.

A BIG VOID IS LEFT

There's a big void in Active Aging this month. It's not white space that you'll notice, but nevertheless, there's a big void on Page 2.

Marie MacDonald, columnist for Active Aging, died December 24, 1992. Marie's Moments has been a part of Active Aging for 11 of the 13-year history of the paper. Her first column appeared in January of 1981 and appeared every month since, except one, April 1987, when she was hospitalized. Her last column, for the January 1993 issue, was written December 10, and the paper had already been printed at the time of her death.

Marie touched the life of anyone she came in contact with and through her column, that number reached into the thousands. Her last column closed with "hug someone, share a little of yourself with others." That was Marie. She spent a lifetime — 82 years — sharing of herself and making her corner of the world a better place. One series she wrote in 1987 comes to mind. Marie opened her heart and soul in a four-part series sharing her thoughts and emotions on the nearly five years her sister spent in a nursing home. It had fallen to Marie to make the decision to put her sister into nursing care and to oversee her sister's care and finances during the next five years. Marie's experiences, shared in four well-written columns, touched many readers and provided good information for others facing that most difficult decision.

I have always considered Marie one of the founding mothers of Active Aging. She was a member of the original Active Aging Advisory Board and served on that board for many years. Even after she was no longer on the board she was an occasional visitor to our meetings and always had a valuable contribution for our discussions.

Two years ago, when she celebrated her 80th birthday, her column summed up just how Marie approached life: " … when I was 35 I expected that by age 60 I would be a doddering old lady, shuffling along in my shawl and house slippers, my eyes and hearing gone, eating milk toast and cream soups (probably through a straw).

"I certainly didn't think that 20 years past 60 I would still be driving a car, cooking my own meals, mowing my own lawn and sitting up past midnight to write this column because I was too busy to write it during the day."

At a time when most are looking forward to retirement, Marie took on new careers. She was ambassador for Cowtown, researching important women from Wichita's past, then portraying them in countless public appearances. She wrote for Active Aging and other publications. She cared for her yard and garden and pets. There was Marie's vinegar works. And more. Every month for the past year, she talked about painting the front porch at Active Aging. And you know, I think she would have done it, if time hadn't run out.

Marie was an award-winning journalist, an able ambassador for Cowtown and Active Aging. But most important, Marie was our friend. We will miss her.

Becky Funke, February 1993